TREASURES OF THE HOPI

TREASURES *of the* Hopi

by THEDA BASSMAN

photographs by GENE BALZER

NORTHLAND PUBLISHING

This book is dedicated to my grandchildren,
Malcolm Maxwell, Benjamin, and Samantha.

Artwork dimensions in photo captions refer to height or length unless otherwise specified.
When two dimensions are given, they refer to height x width.

The display type was set in Matrix
The text type was set in AGaramond
Designed by Rudy J. Ramos
Edited by Kathleen Bryant and Erin Murphy
Production supervised by Lisa Brownfield
Manufactured in Hong Kong by
South Sea International Press Ltd.

FIRST IMPRESSION
ISBN 0-87358-672-7

Library of Congress Catalog Card Number 96-53291
Cataloging-in-Publication Data
Bassman, Theda.
    Treasures of the Hopi / Theda Bassman ;
    photographs by Gene Balzer.
        p. cm.
Includes bibliographical references and indexes.
        ISBN 0-87358-672-7
        1. Hopi Indians—Material culture. 2. Hopi art.
        3. Hopi Indians—Antiquities. I. Balzer, Gene. II. Title.
E99.H7B39 1997
704.03'9745—dc21   96-53291

0617/7.5M/4-97

OTHER BOOKS BY THEDA BASSMAN

Hopi Kachina Dolls and Their Carvers

The Kachina Dolls of Cecil Calnimptewa Their Power Their Splendor

The Beauty of Hopi Jewelry

Zuni Jewelry, which was co-authored with Michael Bassman

*Treasures of the Zuni

*Treasures of the Navajo

The Beauty of Navajo Jewelry

*Also available from Northland Publishing

Frontis, **TOP ROW:** Salako Taka and Salako Mana Kachina dolls (Bassman, pages 2 and 3; Colton, #117–118; Wright, pages 248–249), 14½ in. high, by Von Saufkie. *Courtesy of Tom and Nancy Juda*

Wicker plaque of Salako Kachina, 13½ in. diameter. *Private collection*

MIDDLE ROW, *left to right:* Pot, by James Garcia Nampeyo. *Courtesy of Andrews Pueblo Pottery*

Miniature coil plaque of Mud Head Clown, 4½ in. diameter. *Courtesy of Anne and Randy Joseph*

Miniature coil plaque of Snow Maiden Kachina, 3½ in. diameter. *Private collection*

Pot, right, by Rainell Naha. *Private collection*

LOWER ROW, *left to right:* Miniature coil plaque of turtle, 4 in. diameter. *Private collection*

Miniature sifter basket, 3½ in. x 2¾ in. *Private collection*

Pot with corn, by Iris Youvella Nampeyo. *Private collection*

Miniature coil plaque of turtle with raised hump, 3½ in. diameter. *Private collection*

Belt buckle of eagle, by Joe Josytewa.

Bracelet with Deer Kachinas, sun, and clouds, by Verden Mansfield.

Bracelet with water symbols and Bisbee turquoise stone, by Harold Lomayaktewa.

Pin of Salako Kachina, by Lawrence Saufkie. *Courtesy of Turquoise Village*

Artists unknown for all baskets and plaques.

Page vi, **COIL PLAQUES:**

UPPER ROW, *left to right:* Crow Mother Kachina, 13 in. diameter, by Tirzah Honanie.Hilili Kachina, 20½ in. diameter, artist unknown.

MIDDLE ROW, *left to right:* Salako Kachina, 19 in. diameter, artist unknown.

War God and corn, 14½ in. diameter, artist unknown.

LOWER ROW, *left to right:* Salako Kachina, 9¼ in. diameter, artist unknown.

Unfinished rain design, 3 in. diameter, by Tirzah Honanie.

Unfinished Salako Kachina, 6 in. diameter, by Alice Kabotie.

Salako Kachina, 12 in. diameter, artist unknown. *Private collection*

Page viii, **KACHINA DOLLS,** *left to right:*

Corn Dance Leader (Bassman, page 31; Wright, page 157), 15½ in. high, by Henry Shelton.

Eagle (Bassman, page 22; Colton, #71; Wright, page 87), 19 in. high, by Randolph Poleahla.

Hemis (Bassman, page 106; Colton, #132; Wright, page 214), 20 in. high, by Aaron Fred.

Unfinished Kachina dolls by Neil David, Sr. *All courtesy of Tom and Nancy Juda*

CONTENTS

▼▼▼

Acknowledgments vii

Introduction 1

Jewelry 7

Kachinas .25

Baskets and Plaques 41

Paintings .53

Pottery 71

Treasures Unlimited 83

Glossary .97

Suggested Reading 98

Index of Artists 100

General Index 102

ACKNOWLEDGMENTS

▼ ▼ ▼

My thanks to the following people who so graciously permitted their treasures to be photographed:

Ula and Lee Beaudry
Shirley and Marvin Bowman
Richard Cordell
Barbara Goldeen and John Selmer
Deborah and Dennis Healey
Roxanne and Greg Hofmann
James Mathew Jensen
Jessica Marie Jensen
Pam and Les Jensen
Anne and Randy Joseph
Tom and Nancy Juda
Martin Link
Von Monongya
Al Myman
Gary C. Newman
Jack and Judy Nieburger
Kim Obrzut
Barbara Poley
Orin Poley, Jr.
Selmer Collection
Rosanda N. Suetopka
Bruce and Marilyn Throckmorton
Marlinda Velasco
And all of the private collectors who wish to remain anonymous.

Additional thanks to the galleries and museums and their staffs who provided me with their treasures and help:

Andrews Pueblo Pottery,
    Albuquerque, New Mexico
Calnimptewa Gallery, Oraibi, Arizona
The Galloping Goose, Prescott, Arizona
Heard Museum Shop, Phoenix, Arizona
McGee's Beyond Native Tradition,
    Holbrook, Arizona
Monongya Gallery, Oraibi, Arizona
Museum of Northern Arizona Gift Shop,
    Flagstaff, Arizona
Museum of Northern Arizona Collection,
    Flagstaff, Arizona
Puchteca, Flagstaff, Arizona
Tanner's Indian Arts,
    Gallup, New Mexico
Turquoise Village, Zuni, New Mexico

My thanks to Gene Balzer, my wonderful photographer, who manages to capture with his camera all that I want to say.

Lastly, to my husband, Michael, who is always ready to be my much needed helper, I give my heartfelt thanks.

Introduction

THE HOPI INDIANS are the only Pueblo Indians in Arizona. The current Hopi population includes approximately ten thousand on the Hopi reservation and an estimated five thousand to seven thousand who live off-reservation. The Hopis occupy twelve villages in northern Arizona covering 1.5 million acres at an elevation of up to 7,200 feet. Their land is about one hundred miles east of the Grand Canyon and sixty miles north of Winslow, Arizona.

The twelve villages are on and at the base of three mesas. On the top of First Mesa are Hano (Tewa), Sichmovi, and Walpi. Polacca is at the foot of this mesa. Sipaulavi, Mishongnovi, and Shungopavi are on Second Mesa to the west. Still further west, Oraibi, Hotevilla, and Bacavi comprise Third Mesa, with Kykotsmovi at its foot. (Oraibi has the distinction of being the oldest continuously inhabited village in the United States.) Lastly, Moenkopi, built on the site of ancient ruins, is forty miles to the west of the three mesas.

The land of the Hopis is extremely arid with an annual rainfall of only ten to thirteen inches. Consequently, their

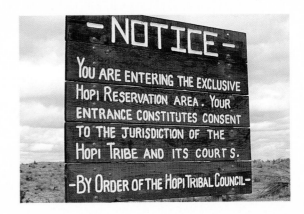

crops require water from hidden springs, rain, and snow. The lack of water has encouraged the Hopis to discover and learn the art of dry farming. Agriculturalists from all parts of the world come to the mesas to study and experience the successful Hopi techniques. The Hopis believe that rain is the God of Life to their arid region.

The Hopis are extremely spiritual people, steeped in traditional ways. They maintain and guard their way of life in spite of the Anglo world that surrounds them. The Hopis are tightly knit through their numerous clans. They are unique among Native Americans in that they live in the "old ways" more than any other North American tribe.

In the early 1600s the Spanish missionaries attempted to eliminate Indian religion in the Hopi villages as well as in the pueblos of New Mexico. They built a church near old Shungopavi, at the foot of Second Mesa. For years the people of Shungopavi were slaves of the Franciscan priests, who forced them to carry large logs a distance of seventy miles from the San Francisco Peaks, near Flagstaff, Arizona, for use as church roof beams. With the church completed, Spanish oppression became even worse. The Hopis were banned from performing any of their own religious ceremonies, the same situation that existed in the New Mexico pueblos. This gave rise to the Pueblo Rebellion of 1680. Together, the Hopi Indians and the Pueblo Indians of New Mexico killed the priests, destroyed the churches, and burned their books and records. They wiped out every trace of the hated Spanish priests and soldiers.

The pueblos retained their independence for nearly twelve years. However, in 1691, the Spanish reconquered New Mexico. At the same time the inhabitants of Awatovi, a Hopi village, welcomed back the priests. The rest of the Hopi villages were aghast at this effrontery to their moral code of fairness and decency. In a rare display of violence the Hopis attacked Awatovi in 1700 and killed all the Christian men—white and Hopi alike. Then the Hopis removed all the women and children to other villages and razed the Pueblo. Awatovi has lain in ruins ever since. This action effectively ended Christian dominance over the Hopis.

The Hopis actively engage in ceremonies whose primary aim is to produce rain, fertility, and growth. To achieve these goals the Hopis may offer prayer sticks, build an altar of sacred objects, pray, sing, and dance. These religious activities are part of everyday living.

The Hopi Kachina dance ceremony is a prayer performed with the greatest of reverence, as well as a dramatic presentation. It is as beautiful as a modern ballet, with exacting footwork and control of body and breath. The dance is full of tricky changes of tempo and rhythm. It looks deceptively easy because each dancer has trained for years and has practiced intensively for days for each performance.

Almost all of the Hopi men perform Kachina dances and the ceremonies that are part and parcel of the Kachina cult. For them, it is a most satisfying and rewarding display of their traditional culture. It is also a time of exhilaration, for the Hopis feel that when they impersonate a Kachina, they become the spirit of that Kachina. As supernaturals they are capable of asking the Kachina spirits to bring clouds and rain, to help the growing of the crops, and to maintain order in the Hopi world. Such an innate sense of well-being and strength!

In each village one or more pairs of tall ladder poles stand out against the horizon. A ladder leads from an opening in the roof down to the kiva, an underground ceremonial chamber. Even though the kiva is used for ceremonial purposes, it also functions as a men's club that is open to its clan members. Sometimes neighbors and members of related clans will also assemble there. Young boys of ten or twelve years of age who have been initiated into the tribal Kachina Society are permitted to join the men in the kiva. The children must be able to keep a secret because at the end of a ceremony they see the Kachina dancers without their masks for the first time. The unmasking of the dancers changes dearly held childhood illusions. That moment is often recalled as an important rite of passage.

It is in the kiva that the boys learn from the men what is expected of them as they grow to manhood, what standards they must aspire to. The men talk to them about honesty, gentleness toward children, and respect toward older persons. The interplay between the young and the old is one of the meaningful activities of a kiva. The ladder poles certainly lead to more than a secluded room.

Among the Hopi people the family plays a significant role. The Hopis are a matriarchal society. It is the woman who is at the head of the house, and the children take their clan identity from her. The father is respected, but it is the mother who holds a position that is different in kind and degree. The woman owns the house, the household goods, and the seeds that are planted every spring. It is the girl-child who perpetuates the clan. The man owns the fields and whatever vehicles they have.

A Hopi household consists of all the blood relatives, near and remote. It also joins with other households that share a common origin. This more extended group constitutes a clan. When a couple marries, the man goes to live in his wife's village. Both the husband and wife have mutual obligations, yet each retains independence. The man may work in the fields, or participate in religious ceremonies, but it is the matriarch of the clan who is the driving force of the family.

The Hopi woman is very busy. There is a home to keep in order, meals to prepare, corn to be ground, instructions and rituals to convey to the young woman to be married, the making of the plaques, baskets, and pottery, and the making of piki, a ceremonial bread. The husband makes a piki stone, which is a stone grill, for his wife. It takes considerable time, care, and skill to produce the piki stone. It must be ground to a fine degree of smoothness, impregnated with the oil of watermelon seeds, and slow-burned or cured before it is ready for use. The woman makes the piki on this stone. First, she builds a very hot fire under the

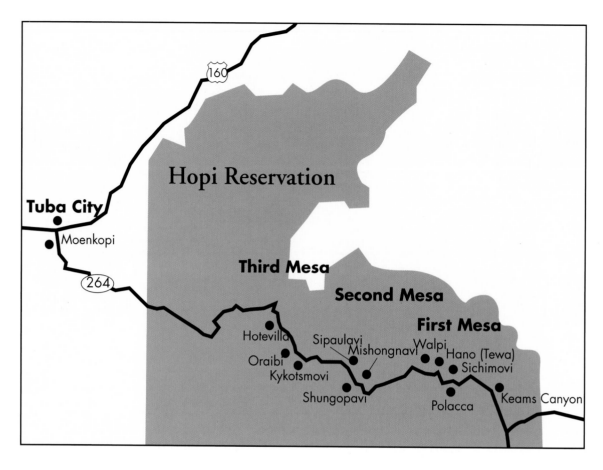

stone. Next, she dips her hand into a watery cornmeal mixture, runs it lightly over the stone with two fingers, and then quickly picks it up and rolls the "bread," which is paper thin. She makes many rolls of piki and stacks them up on a handmade woven piki tray (see page 31). This forms a colorful addition to the table of ceremonial foods.

The Hopis are dignified and friendly people who place great importance on education. Their children in reservation day schools can boast an average daily attendance of ninety percent. It is no wonder the families proudly display photographs of their young people wearing graduation caps and gowns.

Today almost every Hopi family owns a car or truck. Propane gas and electricity

for the homes are readily available in most villages. The Hopis are no longer isolated from the world. They are no longer threatened by starvation from crop failures and drought. Roads, supermarkets, and television are part of everyday Hopi life. Modern industrial and commercial life in the nearby cities of Flagstaff, Winslow, Holbrook, and Phoenix answer many of their physical needs.

Despite the many technological changes, the Hopis steadfastly reaffirm the values of their traditional heritage. They continue to use their own language, insist on practicing their own religion and ancient ceremonies, and carry on their culture in spite of numerous changes brought to the mesas by interlopers and intruders in the past five hundred years. They are determined to live in their own way, the Hopi way. Essentially the Hopis are a conservative, traditional people who have managed to maintain their way of life against mammoth odds. Their oneness with the universe, oneness with the earth, and oneness with all living things makes the Hopi appear to be on a first-name basis with all these components. The Hopis believe all of nature must be in balance and in harmony. In their prayers they pray not only for themselves, but also for everyone in the world so that harmony will exist everywhere. It is not accidental nor an aberration that their very name, *Hopi,* means "people of peace."

Today the Hopis produce more varied types of crafts than any other Native American tribe. Over seventy percent of the Hopi people earn part of their income from making jewelry, plaques and baskets, paintings, pottery, and Kachina dolls. The quality of their work has become finer; there is little likelihood that the knowledge and skill to create these arts and crafts will die out. Among the Hopis, the artisans are not treated as a special people, because the Hopis believe everyone is capable of such work. The degree of proficiency is certainly varied, but artists are not unique. The Hopis design and paint their own ceremonial masks, their Kachina dolls, their pottery. They weave the wedding garments, the sashes and belts. The children are surrounded by relatives and neighbors who produce all kinds of artwork. The children view these objects of great beauty daily, and when the timing is right, many of them will take the first steps to become artists in their own right.

Winter at Walpi village on First Mesa.

Photo was taken in 1968 with permission of the governor of the village.

Jewelry

IN 1898 SIKYATALA, who lived in Sichmovi on First Mesa, was the first Hopi to learn the craft of silversmithing. He was taught by Lanyade, a Zuni, who was the first of his tribe to take up the craft.

FROM YEARS PAST:

UPPER ROW, *left to right:* Bracelet with Persian turquoise, horned toad, and Hopi life cycle design, by Manuel Hoyungowa.

Bracelet with turquoise and coral with bear and heart-line design, by Manuel Hoyungowa.

MIDDLE ROW, *left to right:* Belt buckle with Deer Kachina, by Manuel Hoyungowa.

Bracelet with coral stone, Kokopelli Kachina, corn and pottery design, artist unknown.

Bola tie with bear with heart-line and bear paw, by Manuel Hoyungowa.

LOWER ROW: Necklace and matching earrings with bear paw design, artist unknown.

All made in the 1970s. *Courtesy of Tanner's Indian Arts*

Lanyade visited the Hopi reservation to make silver for sale and trade. He stayed at First Mesa for four months, living with Sikyatala. It was there that Sikyatala observed Lanyade at work. When Lanyade left to go back to Zuni, Sikyatala bought tools of his own and began crafting silver. Sikyatala was also instrumental in teaching other Hopis to craft silver. With regard to design, there was nothing distinctive about Hopi silver. In general, the designs were in the style of Navajo and Zuni patterns of the time.

Overlay began to emerge as a Hopi style in the late 1930s and 1940s, due to the encouragement of Mary Russell Colton, who cofounded the Museum of Northern Arizona in Flagstaff with her husband,

Dr. Harold Colton. She wanted the Hopis to create a unique style by using the overlay technique and adopting designs found on traditional Hopi pottery. There was no immediate success in this endeavor, but the seed of an idea was planted. After World War II ended, returning Hopi veterans were encouraged to enroll in the G.I. training program that began in February of 1947 at Hopi. Fred Kabotie, an eminent Hopi painter, was hired as a design instructor, and Paul Saufkie, Jr., a Hopi jeweler, taught silversmithing technique. Though many design ideas were suggested to the trainees, it was the overlay technique that emerged as the accepted Hopi style.

In 1949, Fred Kabotie organized the Hopi Arts and Crafts Silvercraft Cooperative Guild on Second Mesa. The Guild is still in existence. Hopi veterans enrolled in the classes at the Guild, and by the early 1970s the organization had grown to 149 members. The purpose of the Guild was to furnish materials to the silversmiths, to buy back their finished jewelry pieces, and to sell the jewelry to the general public at a profit, which would be shared with the silversmiths. This plan was devised in order to employ many smiths and to ensure the future production of Hopi jewelry.

A whole panoply of patterns and designs evolved. Traditional Hopi patterns, including the fifteenth-century Sikyatki pottery, furnished a sophisticated, modern look. Hopi patterns were asymmetrical with fluid, curving lines that suggested movement. Hopi decorations contained geometric, spiral, and traditional motifs, such as terraced clouds, religious masks, and stylized animal figures. Then there was the ever-popular Kokopelli, the Hump-backed Flute Player, symbol of fertility, the Casanova of the Ages. At all times there was originality, movement and life, grace, and a contemporary appearance.

Hopi overlay is a two-layer silver technique in which two pieces of silver are formed into flat pieces of the same shape. A design is cut into the top piece with a jewelry saw; the bottom piece is textured and oxidized with liver of sulphur, turning it black. Then the two pieces are soldered together, with the cut-out design as the top. The silversmith sometimes buffs and polishes the surface until it gleams, except for the recessed part, which remains black. More often the silversmith will create a matte or satin finish by polishing with fine steel wool. In the most refined Hopi overlay the seams are flawlessly invisible. Some artists may add a single polished piece of turquoise or coral, but there is virtually no use of stone by the Hopi in overlay. Hopi overlay is primarily an art of silver, or sometimes gold. In 1957 overlay became the tribe's official style of jewelry making. It certainly is the most widely recognized type of Hopi Indian jewelry.

It was Fred Kabotie, manager of the Hopi Arts and Crafts Silvercraft Cooperative Guild, who enthused, "Our objectives are to experiment and test new ideas and techniques in art by using traditional Hopi designs and concepts as well as our own concepts of the inner Hopi." It was Alice Kabotie, Fred's wife, who as secretary-treasurer guided the Guild's fortunes with quiet efficiency.

Just as the opening of the Hopi Arts and Crafts Silvercraft Cooperative Guild was significant, so was the arrival of a private business enterprise, Hopicrafts. Hopicrafts opened in 1961 as an independent shop in New Oraibi (now called Kykotsmovi), owned and operated by two Hopi brothers, Wayne and Emory Sekaquaptewa. They hired Eldon James and Bernard Dawahoya as silversmiths, and Peter Shelton as a designer. Hopicrafts produced jewelry that was distinguished by its superior workmanship, with close attention given to the smallest detail and finish. This excellence in workmanship included texturing the bottom piece of silver in such a manner that it could retain the blackening agent much better, and using steel wool in final polishing to create an elegant satin sheen finish. In addition, Hopicrafts stressed originality in designs.

As a consequence of Hopicrafts' excellent workmanship, there was an upgrading of standards and quality in all Hopi jewelry making throughout the reservation. Designs were clean and balanced, with the use of symbols from past traditions. Bear paws and badger paws denoted Hopi clans; corn stalks and rain clouds represented fertility and growth; Kachina figures and kiva steps were emblematic of the rich ceremonial life of the Hopis. The jewelry exhibited an internal harmony that suggested the serenity of the Hopis.

Since finely crafted Hopi jewelry enjoyed prestige and respectability, the resulting demand for Hopi silversmiths was high. The making of Hopi jewelry truly became an industry, with a phenomenal growth in the number of silversmiths. The work was also a catalyst in augmenting income, so many Hopis became economically self-sufficient. Today a Hopi silversmith can set his own working hours, allowing him to tend his fields as well as take part in ceremonial rites. As time went on, Hopi women learned the skilled techniques of Hopi jewelry making, albeit in few numbers.

Startling and exciting changes took place in Hopi silversmithing when Charles Loloma and Preston Monongye made their entrance into the world of contemporary design. Loloma's combinations of methods and materials are outstanding. These qualities, in addition to an unsurpassed originality in design, raised his work to recognition on an international level. Monongye's jewelry also embodies techniques and materials in a style that went beyond traditional Hopi silversmithing limits. The jewelry of Charles Loloma and Preston Monongye, as well as that of contemporary native artists Victor Coochwytewa, Phillip Honanie, Watson Honanie, Duane Maktima, Philbert Poseyesva, Sonwai, Charles Supplee, Roy Talaheftewa, and Cheryl Marie Yestewa, is acknowledged as "art by Indian artists" rather than simply "Indian Art." Their jewelry draws on native cultural heritage and traditions for inspiration. It is not inhibited by the old, previously established boundaries.

Watson Honanie, known for his work in gold, learned overlay technique from his brother, Phillip Honanie. His encouragement came from two uncles, Fred Kabotie and Porter Timeche. His designs are adaptations from Pueblo pottery and Kachinas, and they portray Hopi culture and ceremonial life.

Philbert Poseyesva lives in Kykotsmovi on Third Mesa, where he learned about silversmithing from Glenn Lucas. He mixes traditional motifs of corn, rain, eagles, and sun with vivid colors of Mediterranean coral and Lone Mountain turquoise. He incorporates gold and silver in his overlay. The asymmetry of his designs highlights their details in a fresh and novel way.

Victor Coochwytewa is one of the premier Hopi silversmiths. He is a traditionalist and a religious leader. He works in his fields every morning, raising corn primarily. In the afternoon he works on jewelry, and in the evening it's back to the fields. There is corn every year, an actuality that pleases him immensely. He has long maintained that corn is his work and jewelry is his hobby. Be that as it may, his jewelry is highly sought after by collectors and his talents are widely acclaimed.

Charles Loloma and Preston Monongye stand out as the two prime, innovative artists of contemporary Hopi jewelry. Preston

Monongye said that he was a traditionalist rather than a modernist. Preston's mother was a California Mission Indian and his father was a Mexican. When he was seven years old, they moved to the Hopi Reservation, where he was adopted by a Hopi family and attended reservation schools. At the age of nine he began his apprenticeship in silvercrafting under the tutelage of his Hopi uncle, Gene Pooyouma. Preston described his uncle as one of the finest men he ever knew. His uncle taught him to love his work and to live the "Hopi Way." Preston's Hopi ties had a solid base. He also felt that old Indian jewelry was great when made years ago, but so were the pieces made by his contemporaries. Though his primary expression was jewelry, he also excelled in other media such as painting, sculpture, and engravings on zinc. Whatever medium he used, he felt that his work was a reflection of the beauty of Hopi culture.

It was Charles Loloma who shook the world of art with his revolutionary ideas in jewelry making. Before Charles, there was no one who dared venture beyond known tribal styles. He broke down barriers as to what an artist could create. He made whatever he wanted to make, with each piece representing the energy and spirit he had at that moment. While working on his numerous jewelry orders, it was his goal to incorporate each particular customer or person in the piece, to portray a quality that even the person may not have known was there. He called these "the inner gems." He felt that these qualities were the parts each of us kept inside ourselves and showed only to a few people. He set the inner gems on the inside of a ring or bracelet, or on the backside of a pendant or buckle. He thought of this inside lining as the lining of the soul. He often claimed that what was inside a person was more beautiful than what we see on the surface. For Charles Loloma, the search for beauty and the expression of that beauty was paramount.

Therefore, it is not surprising to discover that *loloma* is the masculine form of the Hopi word for "beauty" and that it can also be translated as "many beautiful colors." Charles Loloma saw beauty everywhere on the mesas: in the landscape of Hotevilla on Third Mesa where he was born and lived, in the corn-fields, in the blue skies, in the Arizona sunsets. All of this beauty was translated into exquisite jewelry through the originality of his designs, and through the judicious use of gold, silver, turquoise, coral, and jet, or exotic stones and materials such as ivory, ironwood, diamonds, pearls, and lapis lazuli. Charles Loloma became internationally recognized.

In 1980 Loloma studied with Pierre Touraine, a French jeweler living and working in Scottsdale, Arizona. Touraine taught him the use of diamonds and gemstones. Loloma admired Touraine for his ability to breathe life into gemstones and to impart that knowledge and skill to him. Touraine also instructed Hopi artists Charles Supplee and Phillip Honanie. Supplee has said that Touraine taught him about the spiritual fluidity of metal, that making jewelry is infusing life into metal, warmth into cold.

Loloma was responsible for training and working with his nieces—Verma Nequatewa and her sister, Sherian Honhongva—who were born and raised in Hopi. Nequatewa began working with Loloma about 1970; Honhongva joined them ten years later. They served a classic apprenticeship, learning the nuts and bolts of jewelry making by sandcasting, grinding stones, and performing basic yet essential tasks. They watched Loloma at work; he guided them when they worked on more advanced levels. Nequatewa related that Charles taught them beauty may often be hidden, but it's there all around them—outside and inside. He told them there was really no limit to beauty. That is what art was to him.

At the end of the 1980s, Loloma retired from the everyday workplace in the art world. The sisters consolidated what their uncle had taught them, infused those lessons with their own visions, and created jewelry that was not Loloma. It was jewelry signed with the Hopi name, Sonwai. It is fitting that in the Hopi language the female form of the word "beauty" is *Sonwai*.

A collector or purchaser of Hopi overlay work should examine how well the design has been cut. A wavering line or lopsided design indicates an inexperienced or careless silversmith. The design's complexity should also be considered. Some designs, such as a concentric maze pattern, will quickly expose even the slightest wavering. In addition, the recessed areas that have been textured with clean and precise stampwork will heighten or exaggerate the design's contrast and will give the piece an added dimension.

There are always some people who lament the passing of the "good old days" that produced fine old silverwork. But the facts will bear out that more fine work is being produced today than ever before. This is undoubtedly the result of new and better tools, and also because the silversmith is constantly striving to improve designs and techniques. The work of Dinah and Bueford Dawahoya, Joe Josytewa, Marsha Josytewa, Raymond Kyasyousie, McBride Lomayestewa, Duane Maktima, Verden Mansfield, Vern Mansfield, Lawrence Saufkie, Milson Taylor, and Roy Taleheftewa amply illustrate that present-day Hopi silversmithing is alive, well, and flourishing.

NOTE: *All jewelry is sterling silver unless otherwise noted. All gold is 14-karat unless otherwise noted.*

Sidney Secakuku cutting an overlay design as he creates a piece of silver jewelry.

FROM YEARS PAST, *left to right:*

Belt with conchas on leather, made in 1920 by Frank Nutima.

Bow guard of brass and copper on leather, made in 1962 by Glenn Lucas.

Pin of Broad-faced Kachina, made circa 1973 by Norman B. Honie.

Bola tie in shadow box design with turquoise and coral stones, designed by Fred Kabotie and made by Ted Wadsworth in 1973.

Belt buckle inlaid with mother-of-pearl, ivory, turquoise, coral, and charoite, made in 1978 by Duane Maktima.

Reversible pendant on wood with heavy chain, made in 1966 by Phillip Honanie. One side of the pendant has a figure with one horn, and the other side has a figure with two horns.

Courtesy of Museum of Northern Arizona Collection

FROM YEARS PAST, *left to right:*

Necklace with seven pendants strung on silver beads. Each pendant has a turquoise stone and two wings and tail of a bird. Designed by Paul Saufkie, Jr., and made by Lawrence Saufkie in 1969.

Earrings with turquoise (inside necklace), made in 1932 by Sikiumptewa.

Two rings, butterfly design with turquoise, made 1910–1920, artist unknown.

Necklace with one turquoise stone, made in 1949 by Willie Coin.

Ring (inside necklace) with turquoise stone, made in 1955 by Morris Robinson.

Buttons (also inside necklace) with turquoise stones, made 1939–1940 by Randall Honivisiona.

Courtesy of Museum of Northern Arizona Collection

FROM YEARS PAST:

UPPER ROW, *left to right:* Bracelet with snake and Mud Head Clowns, by Eldon James. *Courtesy of Gary C. Newman*

Watch bracelet with Sun face, by Jacob Poleviyouma. *Private collection*

MIDDLE ROW, *left to right:* Ring with Kokopelli Kachina, by Shannon Lamson. *Private collection*

Ring with bird and prayer feather design, by Loren Phillips. *Private collection*

Pin/Pendant Sun face design, by Billy Rae Hawee. *Private collection*

LOWER ROW, *left to right:* Link bracelet with raindrop design, by Victor Coochwytewa. *Private collection*

Pin/pendant with bear and bear paw design, artist unknown. *Private collection*

All made in the 1970s.

FROM YEARS PAST, *left to right:*

Bola tie made of ironwood and Bisbee turquoise. *Courtesy of Tanner's Indian Arts*

Cast bracelet with Lone Mountain turquoise and coral. *Courtesy of Roxanne and Greg Hofmann*

Cast bracelet with Chinese turquoise. *Courtesy of Tanner's Indian Arts*

All made in the mid-1970s by Preston Monongye.

BRACELETS:

LEFT, *top to bottom:* Water design, by Marsha Josytewa. *Courtesy of Turquoise Village*

Rain and cloud design, by Harold Lomayaktewa. *Courtesy of Turquoise Village*

Parrot design, by Marcus Coochwykvia. *Courtesy of Selmer Collection*

Parrot design, by Verden Mansfield. *Courtesy of Turquoise Village*

Water design, by Lucion Koinva. *Courtesy of Turquoise Village*

Water design, by Pascal Nuvamsa. *Courtesy of Turquoise Village*

RIGHT, *top to bottom:* Water design, by Robert Honyaktewa. *Courtesy of Turquoise Village*

Cloud design, by Dawn Lucas. *Courtesy of Turquoise Village*

Long-haired Kachinas, by Vern Mansfield. *Courtesy of Turquoise Village*

Wolves, moon and stars, by Vern Mansfield. *Courtesy of Roxanne and Greg Hofmann*

Bear paws, by Verden Mansfield. *Courtesy of Turquoise Village*

Water design, by Raymie Namingha. *Courtesy of Turquoise Village*

RINGS:

UPPER ROW, *left to right:* Ring with Kokopelli Kachina, by Leroy Honyaktewa. *Private collection*

Ring with water design, by Jack Nequatewa. *Courtesy of Turquoise Village*

Earrings and pin (below) in seashell design, by Preston Duwyenie. *Courtesy of Heard Museum Shop*

CENTER ROW: Three rings with water designs, by Jack Nequatewa. *Courtesy of Turquoise Village*

LOWER ROW, *left to right:* Ring with Deer Kachina and deer tracks, by Joe Josytewa. *Courtesy of Roxanne and Greg Hofmann*

Three rings (bands) with water symbols, by Guy Josytewa. *Courtesy of Turquoise Village*

CONCHA BELTS, LEFT:

Belt with eighteen oval conchas, each 1¾ in. x 1¼ in., of six different designs consisting of a village scene, Long-haired Kachina, Hump-backed Flute Player, Hopi man smoking a pipe and with corn, Sun face, and eagle, by Dorothy Lucas.

Round belt with twelve conchas, each 2¼ in. diameter, of twelve different Kachinas consisting of *(left to right)* Crow Mother, Eototo, Broad-faced, Koyemsi, Heheya, Corn Maiden, Corn Kachina, Cricket, Kokopölö Mana, Hunter, Dragon Fly, and Corn Dance Leader, by Jack Nequatewa.

Courtesy of Turquoise Village

PIN/PENDANTS, BELOW:

UPPER ROW, *left to right:* Water symbols and prayer feathers, by Fernando Puhuhefvaya.

Butterfly, by Corbin Lomakewa.

Salako Kachina, by Lawrence Saufkie.

Kachin-mana, by Raymie Namingha.

LOWER ROW, *left to right:* Bear paw, by Moody Lomayaktewa.

Broad-faced Kachina, by Fernando Puhuhefvaya.

Eagle Kachina, by Fernando Puhuhefvaya.

Courtesy of Turquoise Village

PIN/PENDANTS, OPPOSITE:

LEFT, *top to bootm:* Water design, by Richard Pawiki.

Bear with pink coral stone, by Harvey Quanimptewa, Jr.

Bear with charoite stone, by Harvey Quanimptewa, Jr.

CENTER LEFT, *top to bottom:* One Horn and Two Horn Priests (on chain), by Victor Coochwytewa.

Kokopelli Kachina, by Duane Tawahongva.

CENTER RIGHT: Water design with coral stone (on chain), by Philbert Poseyesva.

RIGHT, *top to bottom:* Water design, by Marvin Lucas.

Crow Mother Kachina and water design, by Trinidad Lucas.

Courtesy of Museum of Northern Arizona Gift Shop

EARRINGS:

OUTSIDE, *clockwise from upper right:* Long-haired Kachinas, by Julian Fred.

Corn and water symbols, by McBride Lomayestewa.

Sun face, by Leroy Honyaktewa.

Parrot, by F. C. T.

Water symbols, by Trinidad Lucas.

Water symbols, by Leroy Honyaktewa.

Water symbols, by Terrance Kuwanvayouma.

Bear, by Leroy Honyaktewa.

Water symbols and prayer feathers, by Elliot Koinva.

Water symbols, by Trinidad Lucas.

Flower, by Loren Phillips.

CENTER, *top to bottom:* Feathers, by Leroy Honyaktewa.

Corn, by Raymond Kyasyousie.

Courtesy of Monongya Gallery

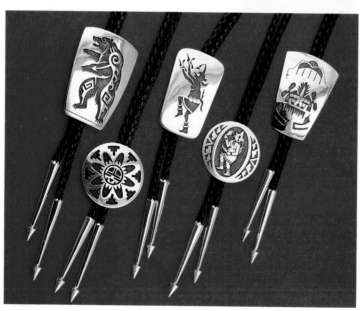

BOLA TIES, *left to right:*

Bear, by Lawrence Saufkie. *Courtesy of Turquoise Village*

Sun face, by Louis Quiyo. *Courtesy of Gary C. Newman*

Mud Head Clown, by Lucion Koinva.
Courtesy of Turquoise Village

Mud Head Clown, by Alde Qumyintewa.
Courtesy of Turquoise Village

Kachin-mana, by George Phillips.
Courtesy of Turquoise Village

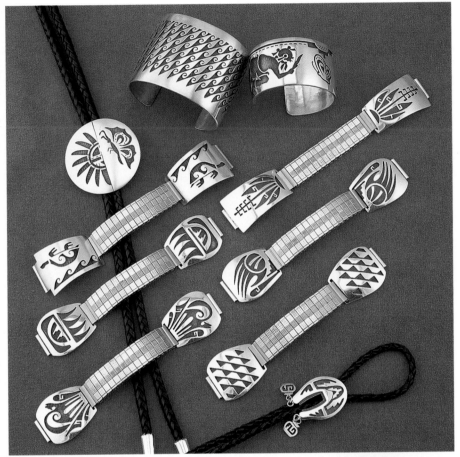

Clockwise from lower left: Watchband with water symbols, by Lucion Koinva.

Watchband with prayer feathers, by Lucion Koinva.

Watchband with water symbols and turtle, by Raymond Kyasyousie.

Bola tie with sun and butterfly, by Edward Lomahongva.

Bracelet with water symbols, by Phillip Honanie.

Bracelet of Mud Head Clown and butterfly, by Emery Holmes.

Watchband with prayer feather, by Lucion Koinva.

Watchband with badger paws, by Lucion Koinva.

Watchband with water symbols, by Lucion Koinva.

Bola tie with water symbols, by Berra Tawahongva.

All courtesy of Monongya Gallery, except bracelets, courtesy of Barbara Poley

UPPER ROW, *left to right:* Cross design hair piece, by Leon Lomakema.

Long-haired Kachina hair piece, by Leon Lomakema.

MIDDLE ROW, *left to right:* Roadrunner key holder, by Julian Fred.

Mud Head Clown key holder, by Perry Fred.

Water design key holder, by Andrew Saufkie.

Water design key holder, by Andrew Saufkie.

LOWER ROW, *left to right:* Corn design cuff links, by Dawn Lucas.

Bear and bear paw money clip, by Dawn Lucas.

Water design money clip, by Andrew Saufkie.

Sun face money clip, by Merle Sehongva.

Bear paw design cuff links, artist unknown.

Courtesy of Turquoise Village

MAZE DESIGNS:

UPPER ROW, *left to right:* Bracelet, made by Vern Mansfield. *Courtesy of Turquoise Village*

Bracelet, made by Alvin Sosolda (a Pima married to a Hopi). *Courtesy of Turquoise Village*

Bracelet, made by George Phillips.
Courtesy of Turquoise Village

SECOND ROW, *left to right:* Belt buckle, made by Philbert Poseyesva. *Courtesy of Selmer Collection*

Belt buckle, made by George Phillips.
Courtesy of Turquoise Village

THIRD ROW: Pendant, by Alvin Sosolda.
Courtesy of Turquoise Village

Earrings, artist unknown. *Courtesy of Selmer Collection*

LOWER ROW: Pin/pendant, by Fernando Puhuhefvaya. *Courtesy of Turquoise Village*

Earrings, by Alvin Sosolda. *Courtesy of Turquoise Village*

Reversible pendant, by Joe Josytewa.
Courtesy of Turquoise Village

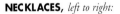

BELT BUCKLES:

LEFT, *top to bottom:* Kokopelli Kachina and corn, by Moody Lomayaktewa. *Courtesy of Turquoise Village*

Snakes, by Fernando Puhuhefvaya.
Courtesy of Roxanne and Greg Hofmann

Parrot design, by Glenn Lucas.
Courtesy of Ula and Lee Beaudry

Eagle, by Ruben Saufkie. *Courtesy of Turquoise Village*

Eagles and sun, by Verden Mansfield.
Courtesy of Turquoise Village

RIGHT, *top to bottom:* Snake dancer, by Vern Mansfield. *Courtesy of Turquoise Village*

Long-haired Kachinas and corn, by Perry Fred. *Private collection*

Sun face, by Leroy Honyaktewa.
Courtesy of Turquoise Village

Ho-ó-te and Long-haired Kachina, by Ronald Wadsworth. *Courtesy of Turquoise Village*

Hump-backed Flute Players and pueblo, by Dinah and Bueford Dawahoya. *Courtesy of Turquoise Village*

NECKLACES, *left to right:*

Single strand of opal beads with sugilite and gold cones and chain.

Triple strand of Red Mountain turquoise beads with spiny oyster shell and lapis lazuli.

Single strand of moonstone beads with gold cones and chain.

Single strand of malachite beads with sugilite and gold cones and chain.

All made by Cheryl Marie Yestewa.
Courtesy of Museum of Northern Arizona Gift Shop

GOLD ON SILVER BRACELETS

TOP: Gold on silver with corn and butterflies, by Raymond Kyasyousie.

BOTTOM, *left to right:* Cast, gold on silver with bear paw and turquoise stone, by Roy Talaheftewa.

Gold on silver with feather design, by Raymond Kyasyousie.

Gold on silver with Long-haired Kachinas, by Raymond Kyasyousie.

All silver with sugilite stone and water wave design, by Cedric Kuwaninvaya.

Courtesy of Monongya Gallery

ALL GOLD

TOP, *left to right:* Bracelet and matching ring, 18-karat gold with coral, charoite, turquoise, fossilized ivory, and lapis lazuli, by Charles Loloma.

Split-twig pendant, gold with diamond, by Charles Supplee. Split-twig figurines were originally made of wood and were first discovered in 1933 in a side canyon in the Grand Canyon. They are estimated to be 2,500 to 8,000 years old.

Bracelet, gold with charoite, coral, sugilite, and lapis lazuli, by Sonwai.

Pendant, gold with pink coral, turquoise, charoite, and sugilite, by Sonwai.

BOTTOM: Earrings, gold with turquoise, coral, lapis lazuli, and pink coral, by Sonwai.

Private collection

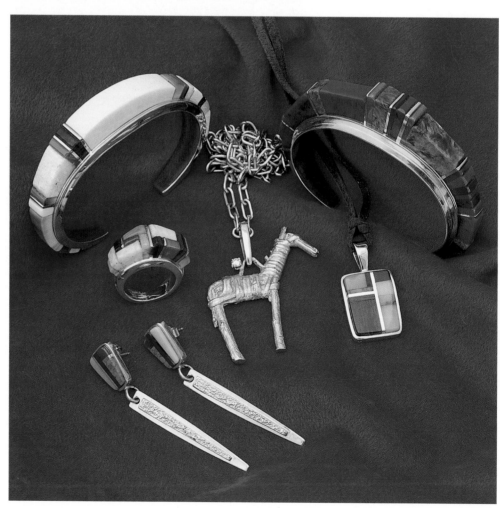

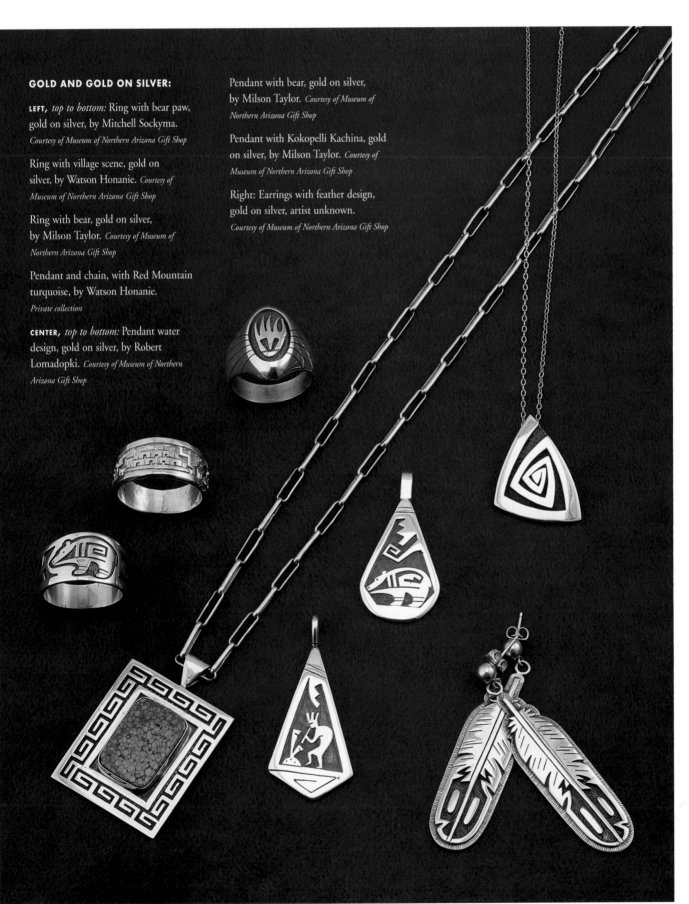

GOLD AND GOLD ON SILVER:

LEFT, *top to bottom:* Ring with bear paw, gold on silver, by Mitchell Sockyma. *Courtesy of Museum of Northern Arizona Gift Shop*

Ring with village scene, gold on silver, by Watson Honanie. *Courtesy of Museum of Northern Arizona Gift Shop*

Ring with bear, gold on silver, by Milson Taylor. *Courtesy of Museum of Northern Arizona Gift Shop*

Pendant and chain, with Red Mountain turquoise, by Watson Honanie. *Private collection*

CENTER, *top to bottom:* Pendant water design, gold on silver, by Robert Lomadopki. *Courtesy of Museum of Northern Arizona Gift Shop*

Pendant with bear, gold on silver, by Milson Taylor. *Courtesy of Museum of Northern Arizona Gift Shop*

Pendant with Kokopelli Kachina, gold on silver, by Milson Taylor. *Courtesy of Museum of Northern Arizona Gift Shop*

Right: Earrings with feather design, gold on silver, artist unknown. *Courtesy of Museum of Northern Arizona Gift Shop*

Kachinas

THE HOPIS BELIEVE Kachinas are supernatural beings who live on the San Francisco Peaks near Flagstaff, Arizona. The Kachinas are considered benevolent spirits of life, fertility, and growth. As spirit beings, the Kachinas live among the clouds, in springs, high in the mountains, and exert their beneficial influence toward the harmonious growth of the Hopi people and their crops.

The Kachinas, who are intermediaries to the gods, come into the villages to dance and beseech the gods for rain, bountiful

FROM YEARS PAST, *left to right:*

Black Ogre (Bassman, page 128; Colton, #29; Wright, page 78), 26½ in. high, by Kenny Lucas.

White Ogre (Bassman, page 11; Colton, #31; Wright, page 80), 26 in. high, by Jacob Koopee.

Both made in 1970. *Courtesy of Les and Pam Jensen*

crops, and a peaceful life. They also help in many of the everyday activities of the villages. At the various ceremonies they appear in traditional costumes as masked impersonators. With the placing of the masks on their heads, the impersonators are believed to take on supernatural qualities. Each Kachina has a distinctive mask or costume and may have a particular identifying song or cry. The masked dancer wears the body paint and clothing of that particular Kachina. He also wears turtle shell rattles on one leg to simulate the sound of the much-needed water.

The Kachinas are represented also as dolls carved from the dried root of the cottonwood tree. Kachina dolls are depictions of the Kachinas and are not idols to be worshipped. A Kachina doll, known as the tihü, is traditionally a gift to a Hopi girl at a ceremonial dance. It is usually made by the girl's father or uncle. The tihü provides a means of education, and is also a decorative article for the home, hanging on a wall. It can be used as a toy, though that is not its primary intention. Its main purpose is to be a constant reminder of the Kachinas and what they represent. As one prominent carver pointed out, "We must not forget all of the reasons why we carve dolls—the carvers must not forget about their culture."

It is estimated that a surprisingly large number of carvers make a comfortable living through their carving. It is also important to note that each individual carver is limited in the number of dolls produced each month or each year because of the complexity of the work. Also, the carver invariably is doing other things—participating in the dances, raising cattle and horses, or planting and harvesting crops.

The Hopi religion requires a great deal of time on the part of the carvers who take part in the dance ceremonies. The dancers prepare costumes, masks, and rehearse songs and dances. When the Hopi Kachina Cult is busiest—winter and early spring—it is a time when the Hopi economy makes the smallest demand. It is also true that in the farming season—late summer and early fall—the men are free to attend to their crops and other pursuits full time. In this way the Hopis have been able to take care of the requirements of the Kachina Cult and at the same time fulfill the needs of daily life. Both the Cult and the economy

flourish under a system in which neither makes demands that interfere with the functions of the other.

Three main ceremonies are presented by the Hopis. In late December there is the Soyal, or the opening of the Kachina season. In February there is the second great ceremony called Powamu, or the Bean Dance. At this time the world is presumably readied for the new season of growth. Out of the kivas emerge large numbers of Kachinas, protected in their activities by guards and warriors and followed as they walk through the village by the ever-present clowns. During this time every Hopi male child who has reached the age of ten is initiated into the Kachina Cult and readied for his growing season just as the land will be.

In the spring there are plaza dances for the purpose of inducing the growth of corn and for increasing the growth of wild and domestic plants and animals. If all the dancers are alike, portraying the same Kachina, the plaza dance is known as a Line Dance. If there are a variety of Kachinas it becomes a Mixed Dance. In either case, if there are Kachinas who dance apart from the lines, they are known as Side Dancers.

The final great ceremony, the Niman or Home Dance, takes place in midsummer in July as the early corn matures. It is a thanksgiving rite for another season of growth. The Kachinas are thanked for their assistance and urged not to forget their friends, the Hopis. In the final ritual the Kachinas are sent home to their mountain peaks, ending the dance. The kiva chief delivers his farewell to the Kachinas: "It's time for you to go home now, taking with you our humble prayer, not only for our people and people everywhere, but also all the animals, birds, insects, and all growing things. Take our message to four directions that all life may receive renewal by having moisture. May you go your way with happy hearts and sunny thoughts."

Originally the Kachina dolls were flat and rigid. Only the heads were well carved and painted. In the early 1900s, even though there was more realism in the carvings, the Kachina figures still had short, stiff legs and were mainly for hanging on the walls of the homes. In the 1930s carvers attached realistic arms and legs, a head that turned, and knees that bent. These dolls were designed to stand up. From the 1940s to the 1970s the Kachina dolls had more accurately proportioned figures, with lively, realistic action. The doll was usually on a stand or base and adorned with feathers, fur, leather, yarn, and seashells. However, in 1975 the United States Government passed The Endangered Species and Migratory Bird Act prohibiting the use of migratory bird feathers. As a consequence, the artists carved wood feathers in delicate detail, as well as items of clothing and jewelry, even though their first attempts were awkward and unsuccessful.

Today the finest Kachina dolls are all wood-carved. Traditional carving tools are still used, but the repertoire has grown to include chisels, Dremel tools, hand and power saws, pocket knives, X-acto blades, and the revolutionary woodburning iron. The woodburning iron allows the artist to greatly enhance the fine details in clothing,

to highlight knuckles and wrinkles, and to produce feathers that are staggering in beauty and character.

The increased technology has made it easier for the artists to express their feelings in the carvings. Dennis Tewa, an unusually gifted carver, has been able to create more realism, more illusion of motion and action. His doll's garments flow; sashes, kilts, foxtails, and capes seem to respond to the wind or the movement of the Kachina figure. The skilled new, young artists Jimmie Gayle Honanie, D'Armon Kootswatewa, Brian Laban, and Roger Suetopka, understand musculature and body proportion. Fingers, fingernails, veins, hair, and embroidery have reached a higher plateau of realism.

The bases the dolls stand on have often been incorporated into the figure, resulting in a one-piece effect. Brian Honyouti has also taken this to a higher level by painting Hopi symbols and Kachinas on the exposed base surfaces and even carving on the underside of the base.

Color is a symbolic feature of the Kachina mask, and it has largely been maintained because of tradition. Six colors and color combinations indicate the direction from which a Kachina originally came to the Hopi village: (1) Yellow, from the north; (2) blue-green, from the west; (3) red, from the south; (4) white, from the east; (5) grey, speckled, or a combination of all of the above colors, from the zenith or up; and (6) black, from down or the nadir.

Most of the carvers use acrylic paints, sometimes in conjunction with wood stains. Brian Honyouti is generally credited with introducing stains as a wood sealer instead of the white undercoat for paint. He used wood preservers in areas of flesh tones, buckskin, and cotton instead of painting them as other carvers did. He later began to use oil paints instead of acrylic paints. The stains changed the coloration of the dolls; bright colors gave way to a soft, muted appearance. Other carvers followed suit and began to finish their dolls with both stains and paints.

The majority of Kachina dolls are still detailed with fur, fabric, and feathers of the domestic fowl. They are popular with collectors and are also much less expensive than all wood-carved action dolls. Dolls in sculpture form emerged in the 1980s. These dolls had no hands or feet, and the carving followed the flow of the wood. These "sculptures" were often elegant in style. Vern Mahkee, Kevin Horace Quannie, and Wilfred Kaye are prime examples of carvers who have attained excellence and expertise in this style.

The miniature Kachina doll has made an impact in the Kachina market. The consumer who desires Kachina dolls often lacks the space to house a large collection. Also, the cost of miniatures is frequently less. Thus, there has been an increase in the number of miniatures carved.

Even though Kachina dolls were traditionally carved by men, women have begun to carve in the past twenty years and they are doing fine work. The late Muriel Navasie was one such carver whose dolls and miniature dolls are prized among collectors. Mary Shelton also has been doing magnificent miniature carvings. In general, women carve because they have the skills, they enjoy the

work, and they require the income. In addition, Muriel Navasie stated that to her the dolls were still a religious form as well as an art form.

The increased demand for Kachina dolls has resulted in a large number of dolls appearing in the marketplace. At the same time, there has been a huge increase in the number of carvers producing good work. Lawrence Acadiz, John David, Aaron Fredericks, and Leonard Selestewa are but a few doll makers who have made an impact.

Henry Shelton, a Hopi carver for many years, was the recipient of the Arizona Indian Living Treasures Award in 1992. This award, presented to artists sixty years of age or over, acknowledges a lifetime of achievement in the arts. Henry is described as one of the first "action Hopi carvers" and as a realistic carver. His work is housed in the Smithsonian collection. He has shown his work in this country and in many other countries. He feels young Hopis need to understand fully their religious culture, to be active in Hopi ceremonies, and to speak the Hopi language correctly and perpetuate it.

It is estimated that there are between 350 and 400 different Kachinas. This count is not exact, since Kachinas come and go. Old ones are dropped, while new ones are added. Some Kachinas appear rarely. In fact, some collectors, ones who have come in contact with an enormous variety of Kachinas, often ask for nonexistent dolls. If the demand is great enough, somehow the supply will emerge. This is how the field mouse who fought and defeated the hawk in a Hopi folktale became a "Kachina doll."

The tale, *Field Mouse Goes to War,* was published with a Hopi text by Albert Yava and an English translation by Dr. Edward A. Kennard, with illustrations by Hopi artist Fred Kabotie. It was put out in 1944 by the Branch of Education, Bureau of Indian Affairs, United States Department of the Interior, and became the first bilingual reader for Hopi children. A purchaser of the book was enchanted with *The Field Mouse Goes to War* and asked for a "Kachina doll" of him. Demand created a supply, and today the Field Mouse is sold as a Kachina doll, even though he has never been danced as a Kachina, nor does he exist in the Hopi Kachina inventory. Yet many carvers, such as Hyram Namoki, make the Field Mouse.

Humor is no stranger to the Hopi carver. Frequently the carver will evoke laughter with his art, particularly with his depiction of the clowns—the Koyemsi and Koshare. The clowns appear in many of the major ceremonies, providing comic relief for some of the dances. Many clowns are an object lesson in improper Hopi behavior, but they also may serve to cure diseases or function as priests in a Kachina dance. They universally appeal to the Hopi audience, and their humor ranges from earthy to sophisticated and is usually related to contemporary events.

The erotic doll has become popular. To the Hopis, sex and all other natural functions are not taboo subjects. They are regarded as facts of life and receive no special attention. Hopi humor, however, runs to the earthy side, and Hopi clowns may perform acts that the non-Hopi might consider totally obscene. However, these figures are not greeted with embarrassed laughter or snide remarks, but with respect. Both Kokopelli and Kokopelli Maiden Kachinas are given exaggerated importance in the Hopi structure because of the large interest among non-Hopis. Hopi carvers have supplied and will continue to supply these dolls in the most explicit detail as long as there is interest in them.

Like most North American Indian tribes, the Hopis do not have a written language. The word "Kachina" has alternatively been spelled katcina, katsinam, and katzina. However, you choose to spell it, a good Kachina doll has the following characteristics: It is carved from the dried root of the cottonwood tree. It has proper body proportions. Details are delineated meticulously. The doll has fingernails. The doll is portrayed accurately, and the painting and/or staining is precise, with clean lines.

NOTE: *The Kachina names in this section are followed by references (in parentheses) to these publications:*

Bassman, Theda *Hopi Kachina Dolls and their Carvers* Schiffer Publishing Ltd. West Chester, Pennsylvania.1991.

Colton, Harold S. *Hopi Kachina Dolls with a Key to their Identification* University of New Mexico Press Albuquerque, New Mexico. 1959.

Wright, Barton *Hopi Kachinas: The Complete Guide to Collecting Kachina Dolls* Northland Press Flagstaff, Arizona. 1977.

THE FOLLOWING ARE EXPLANATIONS OF THE PURPOSE AND FUNCTION OF THE KACHINAS SHOWN IN THE PHOTOGRAPHS.

Ahöla, the Germ God, is a chief Kachina and represents its spirit.

Ahote, also **Yellow** or **Ho-ó-te,** is a hunter.

Ahülani announces the coming Kachina season.

Apache or **Yoche** represents an Apache warrior.

Butterfly Girl is not a Kachina but a social dancer.

Butterfly Kachina Maiden or **Polik Mana** or **Palhik Mana** is the dancing companion to the Poli Kachina.

Chasing Star or **Planet, Na-ngasohu,** is the spirit of a meteor as it streaks across the sky.

Cross-legged or **Huhuwa** is always ready to help others and to give gifts to the children in the Bean Dance.

Crow or **Angwusi** is a warrior who threatens the clowns into behaving.

Crow Mother or **Angwusnasomtaqa** carries the yucca sticks that the Hú Kachina uses to whip the boys during initiation.

Eagle or **Kwa** soars to the heavens in spirit and tells the gods that the Hopis have completed their ceremonies in proper manner; therefore, the rain should come to the fields.

Great Horned Owl or **Mongwa** watches the clowns and monitors their behavior.

Hano Clown or **Koshare** is a glutton and is always eating the watermelon and piki.

Hano Mana is the second gift given to the children.

Heheyas appear in the Bean Dance.

Hólolo speeds the birth of a child.

Hornet or **Tata-nga-ya** is said to be of Zuni origin.

Kachina Maiden or **Kachin-mana** or **Yellow Corn Girl** sometimes carries yellow corn and sometimes a rasp musical instrument.

Kaisale is a very humorous clown and is popular with audiences.

Kokopelli or **Hump-backed Flute Player** is always trying to entice the women.

Left-handed or **Suy-ang-e-vif** is a hunter.

Mastof represents the Earth God, and his function is procreation.

Mocking or **Kwikwilyaqa** is a clown who makes fun of everyone.

Mud Head Clown or **Koyemsi,** who in the photograph on page 36 is blind, is directed by the Paralyzed Kachina.

Ogre, Black or **Nata-aska** is a monster who frightens the children into behaving.

Ogre, White is also a monster who frightens the children into behaving.

Paralyzed or **Tühavi** is usually carried by a blind Mud Head Clown.

Salako (female) or **Salako Mana** is a leader of the Kachinas and is paired with the male Salako.

Salako (male) or **Salako Taka** is a leader of the Kachinas and is paired with the female Salako.

Screech Owl or **Hotsko** is a hunter of birds and fowl.

Situlilü or **Zuni Rattlesnake Kachina** is a guard.

Skirt Man or **Ota** or **Kwasa-itqa** carries the seed bag of corn and is influential regarding its growth.

Snake Dancer or **Chusona,** who is not a Kachina, asks the snakes to carry the message to the gods to bring rain.

Squash or **Patun** is a runner.

Sun or **Tawa** represents the spirit of the Sun God.

Turkey or **Koyona** is a rare Kachina, and his function is not known.

Velvet Shirt or **Navan** is a very colorful Kachina and is said to be of Zuni origin.

Warrior Mouse, not a Kachina, is from an old Hopi folktale which tells how the mouse saved the chickens in the village of Mishongnovi by killing the hawk that was destroying them.

Wolf or **Kweo** is a hunter of antelope.

Yellow Corn Maiden or **Takus Mana** dances with the Long-haired Kachina and uses a gourd and a stick that emits rasping sounds.

Cecil Calnimptewa beginning the carving of a kachina doll.

KACHINA DOLLS FROM YEARS PAST,
left to right:

Hólolo Kachina doll (Colton, #103; Wright, page 168), 8½ in. high, made in the 1920s, artist unknown.

Ahöla Kachina doll (Bassman, page 148; Colton, #2; Wright, page 9), 28 in. high, dated pre-1920, artist unknown.

Wolf Kachina doll (Bassman, page 127; Colton, #86; Wright, page 164), 24½ in. high, made in 1966 by Walter Hamna.

Butterfly Kachina Maiden flat doll (Bassman, page 49; Colton, #120; Wright, page 106), 11 in. high, dated pre-1940, artist unknown.

Other items: Piki tray, 27 in. x 30 in., made in 1937 by Quo-ma-hong-ka (Great-great-grandmother of Willie Coin).

Wicker basket, 13 in. high x 18 in. diameter, made in 1938 by Ida Qwavenka.

Vegetal dye Chief Blanket, 62½ in. x 49 in., made in 1935 by Heveniyowma.

All courtesy of the Museum of Northern Arizona Collection

FROM YEARS PAST, *left to right:*

Snake Dancer (Bassman, page 8), 18½ in. high, by Henry Shelton. *Private collection*

Cross-legged (Colton, #125; Wright, page 40), 15 ½ in. high, by Clifford Bahnimptewa. *Private collection*

Screech Owl (Bassman, page 15; Colton, #80; Wright, page 92), 17 in. high, artist unknown. *Courtesy of Les and Pam Jensen*

All made in 1970.

Left to right: Mastof (Bassman, page 129; Colton, #6; Wright, page 13), 13 in. high, by Peter Shelton. *Private collection*

Chasing Star (Bassman, page 111; Colton, #148; Wright, page 42), 17½ in. high. by Peter Shelton. *Courtesy of Tom and Nancy Juda*

Mocking (Bassman, page 151; Colton, #107; Wright, page 37), 13¾ in. high, by Roger Suetopka. *Private collection*

FROM YEARS PAST, *left to right:*

Skirt man (Colton, #111; Wright, page 39), 14½ in. high, made in 1972 by Wilson Kaye. *Courtesy of Barbara Goldeen and John Selmer*

Eagle (Bassman, page 22; Colton, #71; Wright, page 87), 22 in. high with a 23-in. wingspan, made in 1970 by Kenny Lucas. *Courtesy of Les and Pam Jensen*

Cross-legged (Colton, #125; Wright, page 40), 12 in. high, made in 1970 by Tino Youvella. *Courtesy of Barbara Goldeen and John Selmer*

Left to right: Great Horned Owl, 25 in. high, by John Poleahla.

Great Horned Owl, 16 in. high, by Jimmie Gayle Honanie, Sr.

(Both Bassman, page 73; Colton, #78; Wright, page 111). *Courtesy of Tom and Nancy Juda*

Left to right: Squash (Bassman, page 82; Colton, #225; Wright, page 236), 10½ in. high, by Art Yowytewa. *Courtesy of Les and Pam Jensen*

Mud Head Clowns (Bassman, page 33; Colton, #59; Wright, page 238), 13¼ in. high, by Orme Nahee. *Private collection*

Turkey (Bassman, page 27; Colton, #208; Wright, page 104), 13½ in. high with an 18-in. wingspan, by Leonard Selestewa.

Courtesy of Barbara Goldeen and John Selmer

Squash (Bassman, page 82; Colton, #225; Wright, page 236), 11½ in. high, by Wayland Namingha. *Private collection*

Hano Mana (Bassman, page 109; Colton, #264; Wright, page 51), 16 in. high, by Vernon Calnimptewa. *Courtesy of Calnimptewa Gallery*

Miniature pottery, by Neva Nampeyo and Priscilla N. Nampeyo. *Private collection*

ABOVE, *left to right:*

Salako Mana (Bassman, page 134; Colton, #118; Wright, page 249), 13½ in. high, by Patricia and Vern Mahkee. *Courtesy of Jack and Judy Nieburger*

Yellow Corn Maiden (Bassman, page 47; Colton, #129; Wright, page 175), 11½ in. high, by Wilfred Kaye. *Courtesy of Tom and Nancy Juda*

Warrior Mouse (Bassman, page 42), 13½ in. high, by Hyram Namoki. *Courtesy of Les and Pam Jensen*

Butterfly Girl, 9 in. high, by John David. *Private collection*

Salako Taka (Bassman, page 134; Colton, #117; Wright, page 248), 14¾ in. high, by Orlando Tewa. *Courtesy of Les and Pam Jensen*

Left to right: Salakos with Sun painted on the sculpture (Bassman, page 134; Colton, #117 and #118; Wright, pages 248–249), 31½ in. high, by Kevin Horace Quannie. *Courtesy of the Galloping Goose*

Salako male and female with Kachina Mother at the base (Bassman, page 134; Colton, #117 and #118; Wright, pages 248–249), 24 in. high, by Vern Mahkee. This sculpture won Best of Class and Best of Category at the Gallup Inter-Tribal Indian Ceremonial in Gallup, New Mexico, in 1989. *Private collection*

MINIATURES:

UPPER ROW, *left to right:* Ahülani (Colton, #164; Wright, page 14), 7½ in. high, by Mary Shelton. *Courtesy of Tom and Nancy Juda*

Kaisale Clown (Bassman, page 89; Colton, #63; Wright, page 243), 7½ in. high, by Mary Shelton. *Private collection*

Paralyzed Kachina and the Mud Head Clown (Bassman, page 107; Colton, #144 and #59; Wright, pages 123 and 238), 4¾ in. high, by Lawrence Namoki. *Courtesy of Tom and Nancy Juda*

Eagle (Bassman, page 22; Colton, #71; Wright, page 87), 6½ in. high with 5-in. wingspan, by Mary Shelton. *Courtesy of Tom and Nancy Juda*

Situlilü (Colton, #211; Wright, page 47), 6 in. high, by Mary Shelton. *Courtesy of Tom and Nancy Juda*

LOWER ROW, *left to right:* Kokopelli (Bassman, page 123; Colton, #65; Wright, page 109), 3½ in. high, by Lawrence Namoki. *Courtesy of Tom and Nancy Juda*

Snake Dancer (Bassman, page 8), 5½ in. high, by Mary Shelton. *Private collection*

Ahöla (Bassman, page 148; Colton, #2; Wright, page 9), 5½ in. high, by Mary Shelton. *Private collection*

Miniature pottery, various artists.

Left to right: Wolf (Bassman, page 127; Colton, #86; Wright, page 164), 12½ in. high, by D'Armon Kootswatewa. *Private collection*

Left-handed (Bassman, page 86; Colton, #95; Wright, page 32), 9½ in. high, by Patrick Joshevama. *Courtesy of The Galloping Goose*

Velvet Shirt (Colton, #171; Wright, page 191), 9 in. high, artist unknown. *Courtesy of The Galloping Goose*

Left-handed (Bassman, page 86; Colton, #95; Wright, page 32), 10 in. high, by Aaron Fredericks. *Private collection*

In front: Seven stages of carving a Squash Kachina doll (Bassman, page 82; Colton, #225; Wright, page 236), 3½ in. high, by Lawrence Acadiz. *Private collection*

RIGHT, *Left to right:*

Crow (Bassman, page 117; Wright, page 158), 12 in. high, by Watson Namoki.
Courtesy of Jack and Judy Nieburger

Crow Mother (Bassman, page 99; Colton, #12; Wright, page 23), 11½ in. high, by Vern Mahkee.
Courtesy of The Galloping Goose

KACHINA DOLLS CARVING KACHINA DOLLS, *left to right:*

Hano Clowns (Bassman, page 5; Colton, #60; Wright, page 239), 9 in. high.

Mud Head Clown (Bassman, page 33; Colton, #59; Wright, page 238), 7 in. high.

Heheyas (Bassman, page 19; Colton, #34; Wright, page 83), 9 in. high.

Hornet (Colton, #68; Wright, page 86), 10 in. high.

All by Sheldon Talas. *Courtesy of Monongya Gallery*

MINIATURE POTTERY, *left to right:* Made by Carletta Ami. *Courtesy of Marlinda Velasco*

Made by Carla Claw Nampeyo.
Courtesy of Monongya Gallery

Made by Sherry Kooyaquaptewa.
Courtesy of Monongya Gallery

Made by Bonnie Nampeyo. *Courtesy of Monongya Gallery*

Left to right: Cross-legged (Colton, #125; Wright, page 40), 11 in. high, by Brian Honyouti.

Yellow Corn Maiden (Bassman, page 47; Colton, #129; Wright, page 175), 13½ in. high, by Dennis Tewa.

Sun (Bassman, page 141; Colton, #146; Wright, page 124), 13½ in. high, by Brian Honyouti.

Private collection

Left to right:

Hano Mana (Bassman, page 109; Colton, #264; Wright, page 51), 15½ in. high, by Ernie Holmes.

Yellow Ahote (Bassman, page 120; Colton, #104; Wright, page 170), 11 in. high, by Eli Taylor.

Eagle (Bassman, page 22; Colton, #71; Wright, page 87), 15½ in. high, by Leroy Hongeva.

Courtesy of Richard Cordell

MINIATURES, *left to right:*

Apache (Colton, #205; Wright, page 145), 8½ in. high, by Vern Mahkee. *Private collection*

White Ogre (Bassman, page 11; Colton, #31; Wright, page 80), 8½ in. high, by Vern Mahkee. *Courtesy of Bruce and Marilyn Throckmorton*

Kachina Maiden (Bassman, page 120; Colton, #133; Wright, page 16), 7½ in. high, by Brian Laban.

Courtesy of Richard Cordell

Baskets and Plaques

BASKETRY IS CONSIDERED the mother of all loom work. The addition of machinery has added speed in many of the hand-work processes of the Indians, but not in the making of baskets. Women's fingers are the primary and most versatile shuttles, and weaving is one technique machinery has not been able to improve upon. Even birds are basketmakers in the building of their nests.

Two elements are found in the majority of basket weaves, a warp and a weft. In general, warps serve as a foundation upon which the weft or filler is woven or sewed. The weft holds the warps together. Warps are the stationary elements, and wefts are the moving elements. Hopi basketmakers use three major weaves—plaiting, wicker weave, and coil weave.

Plaiting, the simplest weave, is a process of crossing warp and weft elements at right angles in order to form the basket structure. However, in this weave, since both elements are active; neither element is a true warp or weft. As a consequence, one element cannot be distinguished from the other, for they are the same in size and shape.

The Hopis produce the most versatile plaited basketry in form and design. Plaited basketry is made on all three mesas and in

MINIATURES:

Pottery by Neva Nampeyo, Priscilla N. Nampeyo, Elvira Naha Nampeyo, and Lawrence Namoki.

Coil plaques and baskets, artists unknown.

All sifter baskets by Peggy Kaye.

Courtesy of Gary C. Newman, Barbara Goldeen and John Selmer, and a private collection

all villages, both for native use and for sale or trading. From a design standpoint, the Hopi ring or sifter basket shows amazing versatility, ranging from simple checker patterns to elaborate twilled figurations. Diamonds or squares are favored in Hopi plaited designs. However, zigzags, crosses, lines, and frets increase the scope of the repertoire.

The Hopis use the plaited ring basket as a sifter to winnow seeds and grains. These baskets hold piki bread, cornmeal, and corn, as well as other foodstuff.

The piki tray is a flat, or almost flat, rectangular piece of basketry used for serving piki, the wafer-thin cornmeal bread made by Hopi women for ceremonial purposes. The plaited area of the piki tray is created by weaving bundles of warp elements over other bundles of weft elements. The material used is sumac.

Wicker weave is the second major type of weave used by the Hopis. This weave is a process in which one or several stiff vertical elements (warps) are crossed by one or more equally or less stiff horizontal elements (wefts). The basketmaker maintains these positions as she constantly turns the evolving basket.

Hopi wicker basketry is woven on Third Mesa, in the villages of Hotevilla, Bacavi, Kykotsmovi, and Oraibi, and also in Moenkopi, located about forty-five miles west of Third Mesa. The materials used are sumac for warps, rabbitbrush for wefts, and yucca for securing the rim. The long

shoots of rabbitbrush are cleaned, dyed, and then tied in bundles and stored until they are used.

In plain wicker weaving, the Hopi basketmaker has brought design to a higher level than makers from any other Southwest tribe. The geometrics include not only the typical horizontal lines, bands, cogwheels, checkers, short diagonals, and other elementary patterns, but also larger subjects such as swirls, belt patterns, and elaborate geometrics. Life forms include birds, Kachina heads or masks, or complete Kachina figures.

A great variety of colors has been developed by the Hopis to dye splints for wicker baskets and plaques. The color range is limitless—reds, greens, yellows, oranges, blues, purples, pinks, and others, with many shades of each. Colors come from native or commercial dyes. Variations in colors or shades result from differences in the length of time spent boiling, soaking, and smoking the material with burning sheep's wool. The smoking process sets and defines colors, intensifies a shade, or completely changes a color.

Even the simplest of wicker plaques has at least three or four different colors. More elaborate plaques will have as many as seven, very often with two shades of the same color. Sometimes the color combinations may sound wild when described, but when they are put together by a skilled, artistic weaver the result is invariably breathtaking. The Hopi basket or plaque stands out, regardless of the number, variety, or intensity of colors.

The Hopi women use a greater variety and abundance of colors in their wicker pieces than is used in any other type of Southwestern Indian basketry. The colors are usually of mineral or vegetal origin, though sometimes commercial dyes are used. The color white is bleached rabbitbrush washed with kaolin clay, while pale green is the natural color of the shoots of rabbitbrush. Dark blue comes from the cultivated black navy bean; purple and carmine, from purple maize; reds, from cockscomb, sumac, or alder; and yellow, from rabbitbrush flowers. Larkspur produces a light blue shade, and cockscomb provides lavender or carmine. In vegetal coloration twigs are dipped in a dye bath. Colors are also produced by smoking the twigs with burning sheep's wool.

Within Third Mesa wicker basketry, there are three basic forms or shapes—plaques, bowls, and wastebasket fashions. Plaques are important in ceremonial use as well as in trade. Designs include life forms such as Kachinas, Kachina masks, birds, butterflies, or a Hopi girl with her hair in whorls at each side of her head.

In the months of September and October the Hopis celebrate their Basket Dance. This dance is open for the public to witness, though it closes during a series of secret rites. The women dance in a semicircle, holding the wicker plaques in front of them with both hands and gently swaying back and forth as they sing. At the end of the dance the plaques are given to relatives as gifts. Plaques are also given away by the Kachinas at the Bean Dance in winter and at the spring and summer Kachina dances.

Plaques are used as an integral part of the Hopi wedding ceremony. Before the wedding, female relatives of the bride make a large number of plaques to present to the groom's family. The plaques brought to the groom's house are called "husband's repayment plaques." This is repayment for the bride's wedding robes, which are woven by the male relatives of the groom. The groom's repayment plaque is also symbolic as a "device for descending upon." The Hopis believe that when a man dies he will ride on his wedding plaque—as on a magic carpet—to the Hopi afterworld beneath the Grand Canyon and from there to go live in the clouds.

The third major type of weave is coiled weave. In this weave the warp can be varied in composition but is stationary and horizontal. The weft, which is single and vertical, envelops the warp and is caught or sewed into the preceding coil to form the continuous and joined fabric of the basket or plaque.

Hopi coiled basketry is woven on Second Mesa in the villages of Mishongnovi, Sipaulavi, and Shungopavi. The materials used are basically galleta grass and yucca, which may be split into very fine elements to form a firm and very round foundation.

The Hopis use partially bleached yucca to obtain a yellow color, or the inner leaves of the yucca to produce a natural green. With the addition of dyed black and red or red-brown, the basketmakers have a variety

Effie Dallas weaving a wicker plaque.

by passing the moving weft through the hole. Sometimes she may also use her fingers or teeth to aid her. In this weaving technique, the weaver keeps turning her sewing direction counterclockwise. That is, she sews from her right hand toward her left hand. The Hopi basketmaker sews so tightly that it is sometimes difficult to count the stitches. The remarkably even coils average about two to the inch.

As for forms of coiled work, the flat plaque is dominant. Bowls may be round or shallow, with straight or sloping sides. In addition, there are bowls that are square and rectangular on top and round or oval on the bottom, and some with two small handles.

Designs in coiled basketry include geometrics, popular Kachinas, Kachina masks, Mud Heads, deer, eagles, various birds, turtles (sometimes with raised humps), butterflies, and floral and star themes. There are also clouds with or without rain, sunburst patterns, full figures, and wedding trays. The Crow Mother Kachina is an extremely prominent figure.

of colors to use in their coiled baskets, although these are not nearly as colorful as the wicker baskets. Yucca is one of the most widely used native plants. The long leaves are gathered in the summer and bleached in the sun, usually until they are white. The yucca leaves are cut into very fine elements, and the Hopis will use a bundle of them as the foundation of coiled baskets.

The coiled basket technique produces an immense variety of forms and designs. The designs are realistic, stylized, impressionistic, and geometric. However, coiling is more a sewing process than it is true basketweaving. The basketmaker uses an awl to pierce a hole at some point in the preceding coil, then secures the current wrapped coil to it

In the choice of materials, in their preparation, and in their application to the variety of baskets, the Hopi woman is knowledgeable and ingenious. No matter what weaving form she chooses, the Hopi basketmaker has intimate acquaintance with the location of the native plants to be used and the times when each element is ripe. Nature determines the proper time to gather the raw materials, and the basketmaker knows when that time has arrived. She also knows about peeling, splitting, yarning, twining, braiding, soaking, and coloring the raw materials.

Materials are usually subjected to some kind of moisture when the weaver is ready to begin her work. The twigs can be buried in damp sand, stored in a pail of water, or, if more convenient, wrapped in a wet towel. The weaver also knows what colors come from what sources. She is, indeed, a fore-sighted artist.

The Hopis have been and still are the greatest basket producers among the Indian tribes. Basketry has died out or is extremely limited among the Rio Grande villages, but it is alive and doing well among the Hopi Indians. In a short few generations of time the emphasis in basketweaving has shifted from utility to artistry. Today's baskets are woven with the emphasis on decoration and fineness of weave.

There has been a lack of individual recognition in the art of basketry, probably because the better weavers are older women who were raised in very conservative Indian homes. Even though it's acceptable to excel, it is considered improper to boast about it. Therefore, these women usually choose to remain unheralded.

Selecting a basket or plaque is very much a personal matter. The following are some points for the purchaser to consider: overall aesthetic appeal; fineness of weave (the rim should be tightly woven to the rest of the plaque); type of materials used; how well the materials are prepared, with uniformity of color and shape; size; complexity of design; and relative scarcity. All of these criteria are usually factored in to determine the price of the basket.

In 1902, in a tribute to the Native American basketweavers, Otis Tufton Mason wrote:

As you gaze on the Indian basket-maker at work, you look about you . . . for models, drawings, patterns, pretty bits of color effect. There are none. Her patterns are in her soul, in her memory and imagination, in the mountains, water courses, lakes, and forests. She hears suggestions from another world.

The merely useful basket has some beauty, but the exalted specimen of handwork is the acme of handskill and taste and leads up to the choicest productions. Its maker must be botanist, colorist, weaver, designer, and poet all in one. But could the windows of her mind be thrown open wide there would be seen the mystic love of her tribe alive and active.

SIFTER BASKETS FROM YEARS PAST

TOP CENTER: Sifter basket with willow ring, 15½ in. diameter.
Courtesy of Richard Cordell

LEFT, *top to bottom:* Sifter basket with willow ring, 12 in. diameter.
Private collection

Sifter basket with willow ring, 12 in. diameter. *Courtesy of Richard Cordell*

RIGHT, *top to bottom:* Sifter basket with willow ring, 12 in. diameter.
Private collection

Sifter basket with willow ring, 4 in. high. *Private collection*

Square sifter basket with metal ring, 11 in. x 11 in. *Courtesy of Barbara Goldeen and John Selmer*

Made in the 1960s, 1970s, and 1980s, artists unknown.

WICKER PLAQUES FROM YEARS PAST:

LEFT, *top to bottom:* Corn cobs, 13 in. diameter. Circles going around, 13 in. diameter.

Hopi belt and Navajo belt design, 15 in. diameter.

Whirls, 12 in. diameter.

CENTER, *top to bottom:* Whirls, 11 in. diameter.

Oblong design, 17¾ in. long.

Caterpillar, 15 in. diameter.

RIGHT, *top to bottom:* Butterflies, 13 in. diameter.

Whirls, 12½ in. diameter.

Butterflies, 16¼ in. diameter.

Embroidered robe design, 13½ in. diameter.

All made in the 1960s and 1970s, artists unknown.

Private collection

WICKER PLAQUES AND SIFTER BASKETS:

UPPER ROW, *left to right:* Eagle wicker plaque, 11½ in. diameter.

Turtle wicker plaque, 13 in. diameter.

CENTER ROW, *left to right:* Forest and clouds wicker plaque, 14½ in. diameter.

Sifter basket, 18 in. diameter.

Sifter basket, 11¼ in. diameter.

LOWER ROW, *left to right:* Sifter basket, 9¼ in. diameter.

Wicker plaque with whirls, 11¼ in. diameter.

Wicker plaque with star and lace design, 11¾ in. diameter.

Artists unknown. *Private collection*

WICKER PLAQUES AND BASKETS:

Plaques range from 11 to 15 inches in diameter. Baskets range from 9 to 15 inches in width and 4½ to 8 inches in depth. Basket on top and basket on left, both bowl-shaped, were made by Tillie Mayestewa in the early 1970s. All other baskets and plaques were made in the 1970s, 1980s, and 1990s, artists unknown. *Two plaques on lower left courtesy of Richard Cordell; all others, private collection*

WICKER PLAQUE AND BASKET:

Unfinished and finished plaques, artist unknown.

Unfinished basket, by Peggy Kaye.

Finished basket, by Adrinne Nutumya.

Grasses on left form the foundation and are sumac or wild currant. Grasses on right form the weft and are rabbitbrush.

Private collection

WICKER PLAQUES WITH FIGURES:

UPPER ROW, *left to right:* Hunter Kachina, 16 in. diameter. *Private collection*

Butterfly, 12 in. diameter. *Courtesy of Richard Cordell*

Mother Kachina, 15½ in. diameter. *Private collection*

CENTER ROW, *left to right:* Cricket Kachina, 13½ in. diameter. *Private collection*

Snow Maiden Kachina, 16 in. diameter. *Private collection*

Crow Mother Kachina, 13 in. diameter.
Courtesy of Richard Cordell

LOWER ROW, *left to right:* Kau-a Kachina, 13¾ in. diameter. *Private collection*

Kachin-mana Kachina, 15 in. diameter.
Courtesy of Shirley and Marvin Bowman

Early Morning Kachina, 12 in. diameter.
Courtesy of Les and Pam Jensen

Artists unknown.

COIL PLAQUES AND BASKETS:

UPPER ROW, *left to right:* Butterfly Maiden, 15½ in. diameter, by Lorraine Secakuku. *Courtesy of Von Monongya*

Kachina Mother, 13 in. diameter, by Dora Sakeva. *Courtesy of Monongya Gallery*

MIDDLE ROW, *left to right:* Supai Girl, 15 in. diameter, by Janet Lamson. *Courtesy of Monongya Gallery*

Eagle, 13 in. diameter, by Lorraine Secakuku. *Courtesy of Von Monongya*

Basket with Mud Head Clowns and Kachin-mana, 8½ in. high, by Maggie Adams. *Courtesy of Monongya Gallery*

LOWER ROW, *left to right:* Basket with Heheya Kachinas and War God, 5½ in. high, by Maggie Adams. *Courtesy of Monongya Gallery*

Basket with Heheya Kachinas and corn, 5 in. high, by Zola Lomakema. *Courtesy of Monongya Gallery*

Cloud design, 9½ in. diameter, by Lorraine Secakuku. *Courtesy of Von Monongya*

Kachin-mana, 10 in. diameter, artist unknown. *Courtesy of Monongya Gallery*

Basket with five Long-haired Kachinas and rain and cloud symbols, 16 in. high and 24 in. diameter, by Madeline Lamson. This basket won Best of Show in the Gallup Inter-Tribal Indian Ceremonial in Gallup, New Mexico, in 1990.
Courtesy of Turquoise Village

Tirzah Honanie demonstrating the weaving of a Crow Mother coil plaque at a gallery showing. Finished plaque is on page vi, upper left.

COIL PLAQUES AND BASKETS:

LEFT, *top to bottom:* Turtle plaque with raised hump and beetles, 11½ in. diameter, made in 1976 by Evelyn Pela. *Private collection*

Basket with rain and cloud design, 2½ in. high, made in 1975 by Beatrice Tewawina. *Courtesy of Martin Link*

Eagle plaque, 10 in. diameter, made in 1974, artist unknown. *Courtesy of Barbara Goldeen and John Selmer*

Turtle plaque, 11 in. diameter, made in 1974, artist unknown. *Private collection*

CENTER, *top to bottom:* Turtle plaque with raised hump, 15½ in. diameter, made in 1975 by Martha Leah Kooyamoema. *Private collection*

Butterfly plaque, 14½ in. diameter, made in 1979 by Martha Leah Kooyamoema. *Private collection*

Plaque with six deer heads, 10 in. diameter, made in 1975, artist unknown. *Courtesy of Barbara Goldeen and John Selmer*

Unfinished plaque with star design, made in 1979 by Tirzah Honanie. *Private collection*

RIGHT, *top to bottom:* Turtle plaque with raised hump, 11½ in. diameter, made in 1979, artist unknown. *Private collection*

Plaque with eagle, 10 in. diameter, made in 1979, artist unknown. *Courtesy of Richard Cordell*

Basket with four deer, 3½ in. high, made in 1974, artist unknown. *Courtesy of Martin Link*

COIL PLAQUES:

UPPER ROW, *left to right:* Eagle, 13½ in. diameter.

Left-handed Kachina, 13½ in. diameter.

Salako Kachina, 10 in. diameter.

Courtesy of Musuem Northern Arizona Gift Shop

LOWER ROW, *left to right:* Rain and cloud design, 13½ in. diameter. *Courtesy of MNA Gift Shop*

Four deer, 11 in. diameter. *Courtesy of MNA Gift Shop*

Mud Head Kachina, 5 in. diameter, by Madeline Lamson. *Courtesy of Turquoise Village*

Turtle with raised hump, 4½ in. diameter, by Madeline Lamson. *Courtesy of Al Myman*

Turtle, 4¼ in. diameter, by Madeline Lamson. *Courtesy of Turquoise Village*

Artists unknown unless otherwise noted.

COIL BASKET FROM YEARS PAST:

The inside bottom of the basket (pictured above) features the Salako Kachina. The figures around the basket are two Eagle Kachinas, two Mud Head Clowns, and two Crow Mother Kachinas, with four ears of corn, and rain and cloud designs. 15 in. high and 18 in. diameter, made in the early 1970s by Lorraine Secakuku. *Private collection*

Paintings

HOPI PAINTINGS ARE a reflection of Hopi life. Fertility rites, rain ceremonies, universal harmony, oneness with the earth, and especially Kachinas are recurring subjects and themes. Almost all Hopi art—petroglyphs, altar hangings, kiva murals, Kachina ceremonies, and modern paintings—includes one or more symbols of water, the source of life. These symbols encompass rain, clouds, tadpoles, turtles, and frogs.

It was Fred Kabotie who was most influential and most highly regarded as a

champion of the traditional form of Native American painting. He was an artist of dominant stature. He was not quite five feet tall, yet he was a giant among men. He was a talented, loving, and gentle man, endowed with immense humor. Quality was always uppermost in his mind. His Kachina ceremonial paintings brought this religious art to its maximum visual impact. His place as a guardian of traditional Hopi culture has never been questioned, never been compromised.

Fred Kabotie was born in 1900 in the village of Shungopavi on Second Mesa, Arizona. In 1920 he went to Santa Fe, New Mexico, where he was employed by the School of American Research. As part of the employment agreement he was allowed to paint two to three hours a day, presumably not subjected to any white influences. It was there he developed his own style and color sense. His themes emphasized native Hopi dancers.

Fred Kabotie could undoubtedly have made a great deal of money from his painting. Instead he chose to teach, to experiment with new ideas, and to work for the progress of the Hopi people. For example, in 1947 he was a major catalyst in inducing the federal government to fund a program on the Hopi reservation, to set up a school to provide returning war veterans of World War II a place to learn jewelry making. He and Paul Saufkie, Jr., conducted the classes from which emerged the Hopi overlay style of jewelry.

Fred Kabotie's artwork was devoted to perpetuating on canvas ancient Hopi customs, rituals, and the most momentous stories of Hopi mythology. In the world of the Hopis it is impossible to separate the activities of daily life, religious observance, and artistic creation.

In the 1920s Kabotie was commissioned by the Heye Foundation of the Museum of the American Indian in New York to paint a series of representations of the Hopi tribal dances. He also did murals at the Grand Canyon of Arizona for the Fred Harvey Company. Fred Kabotie was truly the first Hopi to receive individual recognition as an artist.

In 1937 Kabotie taught art at the Oraibi High School in Arizona. He helped train Hopi students interested in painting. Raymond Naha, one of his students, went on to become a recognized successful painter in his own right. Naha, a Hopi-Tewa Indian, was born in 1933 in the village of Polacca, Arizona. He has produced work in oils, pastels, ink, casein, and in the later 1960s, almost exclusively in acrylics. Naha frequently used dark paper, and his brush tended to emphasize the dark side, as in his painting of masks.

Between 1920 and 1930 another Hopi, Otis Polelonema, arrived on the painting scene. Otis was born in 1902 in the village of Shungopavi. Both Kabotie and Polelonema developed as great Hopi traditional painters. They exerted a tremendous influence on other Hopi artists. Kabotie's significant contribution was in modeling, the creation of an image on a flat surface through the use of color and shading. Polelonema excelled in the depiction of dress as well as in his presentation of the masked Kachina dancers. Otis worked largely in watercolor and oils.

In evaluating Hopi painting through 1970 it is probable that Fred Kabotie, Otis Polelonema, and Raymond Naha were the outstanding Hopi artists. The best Hopi work of that period dealt with Native themes, especially the Kachina, done with shading and perspective by Kabotie and Polelonema. Naha added more action and a greater variety of painting methods.

Waldo Mootzka was born in 1903 near the village of Oraibi, Arizona, and died at an early age in 1941. He did most of his painting between 1930 and 1940. He attended the Indian School at Albuquerque, New

Mexico, though he was there prior to the establishment of their art department. He was, essentially, a self-taught painter, as were some of the first artists. He was primarily influenced by Fred Kabotie. Mootzka's paintings combine artistry with an authentic recording of Indian life. His composition is beautiful, as is his use of traditional symbols. His themes emphasize Kachinas, which he portrays both singly and in groups. He is at his artistic zenith in the painting of ceremonial and mythological scenes that radiate the power of the eternal life cycle. He also painted extensively on the theme of fertility. He simultaneously portrayed the fertility rites for the corn crop and the fertility rites for the propagation of the Hopi people.

In 1932 Dorothy Dunn established an experimental studio in the Santa Fe Indian School to encourage the art aspirations of forty young Native American students. Her efforts resulted in a painting department at the Santa Fe Indian School. The new department was established by the Department of the Interior in December 1933, making it the first time the federal government officially recognized Indian painting. In succeeding years, art departments were established at Albuquerque, Phoenix, Oraibi, and other Indian schools on a secondary level.

Bruce Timeche, a Hopi artist, was born in 1923 in the village of Shungopavi, on Second Mesa, Arizona. He graduated from an art school in Phoenix, Arizona. Much of his painting is in the tradition of the Hopi tribe, as to both subject matter and style. Most of Timeche's paintings relate to individual Kachinas, which he paints in traditional style. He uses oil or tempera. His work is a model of excellence, with outstanding qualities in depth, draftsmanship, shading, and shadows.

Logan Dallas painted a number of Kachinas and landscapes in oils. His Snake Dance at Old Oraibi, painted in this medium, is extremely good. He captures the flavor and feeling of the ceremony beautifully. In 1970 Dallas was painting Kachina and village scenes almost exclusively.

Clifford Bahnimptewa was born in 1937 in the village of Old Oraibi on Third Mesa, Arizona. He had no formal art training, but for a short while he acquired experience at the Phoenix Indian School. His background as a Kachina doll carver helped in his paintings of the human figures taking part in the Kachina dances.

Bahnimptewa did a series of 286 paintings of Hopi Kachina dancers, based on the list compiled by Dr. Harold S. Colton in the book *Hopi Kachina Dolls with a Key to Their Identification*. He worked on this project from 1968 to 1970. His goal was to paint these Kachinas as dancing performers, not as Kachina dolls. He viewed each figure separately as an artistic problem relating to its usual dancing posture. He avoided extreme action poses where they were not appropriate to the particular dance. However, he did use more active poses where these occur in the dances, as well as formal gestures and poses. His paintings exhibited fine detail in color and form, in costumes, body paints, and ceremonial adornments.

Bahnimptewa used watercolor and tempera media emphasizing the power and authority of the Kachinas, their connection with and importance to the crops and harvest. The series is a significant account of one man's understanding of his traditional religion in a time of change. Barton Wright, the renowned authority on the subject of Hopi Kachinas, used 237 of the late Clifford Bahnimptewa's illustrated paintings in the superb book *Kachinas: A Hopi Artist's Documentary.*

In 1973 Artist Hopid was formed. The group of young Hopi artists included at various times Neil David, Sr., Delbridge Honanie, Michael Kabotie, Milland Lomakema, Tyler Polelonema, and Terrance Talaswaima. Their objectives were to experiment and test new ideas and techniques in art by using traditional Hopi designs and concepts as well as their own present-day concepts of the inner Hopi. It was the desire of the Artist Hopid to document Hopi history and events through visual arts. Their works were displayed at the Hopi Cultural Center Museum on Second Mesa, Arizona. Occasionally visitors to the museum would tell Fred Kabotie, "These Hopi painters have been influenced by Picasso." Kabotie answered with a twinkle in his eye, "No, Picasso was influenced by the Hopi."

Artist Hopid's members (as well as many other artists) have painted on the walls of kivas. Some of their works are hanging in museums throughout the world. They truly have made an impact in the art world, and at the same time in defining and clarifying what it means to be Hopi. Individually and collectively, the members of Artist Hopid used their art to instill Hopi pride and identity. Artist Hopid disbanded in 1976 due to financial reasons, but its members are still painting.

One member, Michael Kabotie, is the son of the late Fred Kabotie. He studied art in Oraibi High School under his father, and later at the University of Arizona. When Michael was initiated into Hopi secret societies in 1967, he was given the name Lomawywesa, which means Antelope-walking-in-harmony. Michael was an active member in Artist Hopid from 1973 to 1976. After it disbanded, he divided his time and considerable talent to both painting and jewelry making. His main subject matter as a painter is abstracts with native themes. He works with casein, acrylic, polymers, oils, and watercolors.

Another former member of Artist Hopid, Neil David, Sr., was born in 1944 in the village of Polacca, Arizona, and is a Hopi-Tewa. He works in acrylic, pen and ink, watercolors, and crayons. His subject matter celebrates the ceremonies and the symbols of water and fertility that are extremely important to the Hopis. He uses great detail and bright colors, highlighting costuming and jewelry. Kachinas are high on his list of subject matter. His paintings of seventy-nine Kachinas are beautifully depicted in the recent book *Kachinas: Spirit Beings of the Hopi,* by Brent Ricks and Alexander

Anthony, Jr. In addition to being an excellent painter, Neil is a master Kachina doll carver. In both his drawings and carvings, his clowns are unsurpassed for their portrayal of humor.

Dan Namingha was born in 1950 at Keams Canyon, Arizona. He comes from five generations of potters and artists. His great-grandmother was Nampeyo, the famed potter. Rachel Nampeyo, his grandmother, and Dextra Quotskuyva Nampeyo, his mother, were also extraordinary potters. Raymond Naha, his uncle, was a painter and Kachina doll carver. Namingha did a mammoth mural, an abstract painting that hangs prominently in Phoenix Sky Harbor International Airport. His abstract designs are bold and sweeping, his textures are varied, and his colors are vivid. His work most assuredly carries on the Nampeyo heritage.

David Dawangyumptewa was born in 1962 in the village of Kykotsmovi on Second Mesa, Arizona. He has been painting since 1983. His main influences are the paintings of Walden Lomayesva and Reuben Lomayesva. What spurs him on is his own standard of quality. He maintains that he is his own competition. However, his many awards at Santa Fe Indian Market in Santa Fe, New Mexico, and the Hopi Show at the Museum of Northern Arizona, in Flagstaff, attest to his popularity as an artist. Dawangyumptewa works only in gouache and uses 23-karat gold leaf on handmade paper. He likes gouache as a medium because of its quick-drying property and its brilliancy and vibrancy of color. His paintings are often laced with whimsical, charming creatures.

Michael Lacapa is an illustrator and writer with five books to his credit. He admired the work of his grandmother, Elizabeth Lacapa, and his aunt, Cordilla Pahona, who made pottery. Seeing the fine quality of their work inspired him to take up painting. In his paintings, he uses the imagery inherent in Hopi-Tewa pottery and the style from the Sikyatki revival. He uses the designs to tell the story of ceremonies, prayers, and rituals.

The dominant themes of Hopi painting have been fertility and religious observances, as seen in the Kachina ceremonies. The Kachina world is a microcosm of the Hopi world. The Kachinas have a dual identity. They represent spirits of the supernatural world, as well as men from the world of the living who perform in the Kachina dance ceremonies. This duality of man and mask is a central theme of many Hopi paintings. It is at the core of Hopi life. The individual artist living both on and off the reservation finds his rewards in inner peace and a feeling of well-being rather than in the pride of personal achievement or status as an artist. In the world of the Hopis, daily life activities, religious observance, and artistic creation are indivisible.

FROM YEARS PAST:

Rocky Mountain Sheep Dancers, watercolor, 9 in. x 13 in., painted in 1934 by Fred Kabotie. Depicts four dancers with a leader who is carrying a bow and arrow. *Courtesy of Museum of Northern Arizona Collection*

FROM YEARS PAST:

Untitled, oil, 15½ in. x 19½ in., painted before 1968 by Logan Dallas. Depicts Snake Dancers, pueblo, and spectators. *Courtesy of Museum of Northern Arizona Collection*

FROM YEARS PAST,

Oil, 36 in. x 24 in., painted in 1960s by Raymond Naha. Depicts five Hopi masks and bell ankle rattles. *Courtesy of Tanner's Indian Arts*

Part of the Snake Dance

by Otis Polelonema

FROM YEARS PAST:

Eight Antelope Singers, watercolor, 15½ in. x 22 in., painted in 1930 by Otis Polelonema. To the right is the kisi, a bower of cottonwood in which the snakes are housed before the Snake Dance. *Courtesy of Museum of Northern Arizona Collection*

FROM YEARS PAST

LEFT: *The Mud Head Clown (left)* 9½ in. x 7½ in., painted in 1972, and *Ogre Woman (right),* 9 in. x 7 in., painted in 1974, watercolor, by Clifford Bahnimptewa. *Private collection*

FROM YEARS PAST:

Hopi Bringers of Rain, acrylic, 18 in. x 24 in., painted in 1976 by Neil David, Sr. The Hopi man is throwing cornmeal into the heavens and asking the Long-haired Kachinas to come down and bring rain. When the Long-haired Kachinas bring the rain they lay their long hair on the ground to hold the moisture so that the corn will grow. *Private collection*

FROM YEARS PAST:

Hopi Women's Basket Dance, watercolor,
15¾ in. x 22¾ in., painted 1920–1921
by Fred Kabotie. Depicts forty women holding
their baskets or plaques and two Qaqole Manas.

Courtesy of Museum of Northern Arizona Collection

FROM YEARS PAST:

Koshare Fiesta, watercolor, 20 in. x 13 in.,
painted 1930–1940 by Waldo Mootzka. Depicts
five Koshare Clowns climbing a pole. The Koshares
are called the fun makers. The pole is polished and
greased and whoever reaches the top first may select
any one article from the cross beam as soon as he is
able to carry it down with him.

Courtesy of Museum of Northern Arizona Collection

FROM YEARS PAST:

Lefties out Hunting, watercolor, 17½ in. x
11¾ in., painted in 1959 by Bruce Timeche.
Depicts two Left-handed Kachinas.

Courtesy of Museum of Northern Arizona Collection

FROM YEARS PAST:

Guardian of the Children, acrylic, 11 in. x 13 in., painted in 1976 by Neil David, Sr. *Private collection*

RIGHT: *Emergence of Cloud Woman,* acrylic, 14 in. x 31½ in., by Neal Naha, Jr. Depicts Salako Kachina. *Private collection*

TEWA CLOWNS, ABOVE
AND BELOW: Pen, ink,
and watercolor, 8½ in.
x 14 in., 8 ½ in. x 11½
in., both by Neil David,
Sr. *Private collection*

TOP AND MIDDLE: *Sikyatki Butterflies Symbolic Imagery*, watercolor, both 6 in. x 9 in., by Michael Lacapa.

BOTTOM: *Prehistoric Petroglyph Mogollon Imagery*, watercolor, 5 in. x 8½ in., by Michael Lacapa.

Private collection

Rain Spirits, lithograph, 22½ in. x 15 ¼ in., by
Lomawywesa (Michael Kabotie). This six-color
lithograph was the first of a series of paintings entitled *Kachina Poetry*. Michael Kabotie chose the
Long-haired Kachina because its song calls for rain.
The long flowing hair and beard represent the
falling rain. The designs are abstract symbols
of fertility, lightning, rain, and clouds.

Private collection

LEFT: *Polik Mana Watching the Frogs Go By,* 14 in. x 21 in., by David Dawangyumptewa. This is a seven stone lithograph and is the first hand-pulled color lithograph that David made. It is an edition of seventy-five, with eight artist's proofs. The figure Polik Mana is the Hopi Butterfly Maiden. *Courtesy of the artist*

OPPOSITE: *Midday Sun,* gouache with 23-karat gold leaf on handmade paper, 12 in. x 14 in., by David Dawangyumptewa. This is an afternoon scene with the Kokopelli playing his flute, representing the life and times of the Kokopelli at midday. *Courtesy of the artist*

The Underwater People, gouache, 26½ in. x 10⅝ in., by David Dawangyumptewa. These are the water spirits who live underwater and purify the moisture that falls to Mother Earth. The underwater foliage, water bubbles, and crosses represent the purity of water that evaporates into the sky to once again fall to earth. The majestic sounds from the mosaic-covered drums across the lower part of the painting are part of the music beneath the earth's surface. *Courtesy of the artist*

Pottery

HOPI POTTERY IS made on First Mesa in the villages of Walpi, Sichmovi, and Hano, and in Polacca, which is located at the foot of the mesa. It was largely Nampeyo, a Tewa potter from Hano, and her revival of the ancient Sikyatki ware that were responsible for the development of the modern era of Hopi pottery beginning at the end of the nineteenth century. It was most surely the success and artistry of Nampeyo that encouraged

other women in the villages to turn to pottery as a means of supporting their families. The pottery tradition on First Mesa is strong and healthy, and the future appears promising for its continuation and growth.

Hopi clay, the standard Hopi ceramic material for about six centuries, fires to shades of yellow and orange. Hopi clay is considered probably the finest that is available in the Southwest. When it is fired, it hardens to a dense, tough piece of pottery.

Five hundred years ago the Hopis used this clay to form the artistic pottery style called Sikyatki Polychrome, named for a village that was abandoned before the Europeans came to North America. In the 1890s the archaeologist J. W. Fewkes

UPPER ROW, *left to right:* Pot with bird design, by Rondina Huma.

Pot with bird design, by Tonita Hamilton Nampeyo.

Pot with bird design, by Rondina Huma.

LOWER ROW, *left to right:* Pot with parrot design, by Nathan Begaye (Hopi-Navajo).

Pot with rain and cloud design, by Rondina Huma.

Private collection

and his party excavated the ruins of Sikyatki and uncovered magnificent ancient pottery. Nampeyo's husband, Lesso, worked in Fewkes's project and brought her shards of Hopi pottery that went back to the sixteenth century—the Sikyatki period. These shards inspired Nampeyo to create new shapes and designs. Her innovations have been studied and imitated for seventy-odd years, with three generations of her family continuing the pottery tradition.

Pottery making begins when Hopi clay is obtained by the potters, who know exactly what they want and where they can find it. This is followed by drying, soaking and washing, grinding, sifting, and finally adding temper. The Hopi potter usually does not find it necessary to temper the clay—that is, to add material to the clay to reduce shrinkage and cracking in the drying and firing processes. Hopi clay is considered tantamount to being perfect without the temper.

Hopi pottery is generally made by the coil and scrape method. The clay is coiled upwards to form the walls of the pot and the coils are smoothed as the walls become higher. The scraping tools may be circular pieces of squash rind, parts of gourds, flat wooden sticks such as tongue depressors, or broken pieces of pottery. A well-made pot will be uniform and symmetrical. The smooth walls will be of even thickness from the base to the rim. The more expert the potter, the thinner the walls and the lighter the pot for its size.

A cloth fabric dipped in a solution of water and clay is wiped onto the surface of the vessel as soon as it has reached a leather-hard state. Polishing is accomplished with a small water-worn pebble dipped in water from time to time. The pebble is rubbed over the surface of the vessel until the desired shine is produced. At that point the pot is ready for the painting of the designs. Paintbrushes are traditionally made from the leaves of narrowleaf yucca, but some potters buy brushes in art supply stores. The Hopi women are most distinguished as painters. They are considered the preeminent masters of fine line.

When the design is completed and the paint is dry, the pot is ready for firing. The firing is always done in the open. A fire is made of sheep dung piled on juniper wood chips. The blocks of sheep dung are obtained from the Navajos. Cedar and native coal are sometimes used as well. A sandstone platform or a grate is then positioned over the burning dung. A few large shards from broken vessels are laid on the platform, and the pots are placed in an upside-down position on top of the shards. A dome of large shards to protect the pots from the dung is laid over the pots. The pots are fired for several hours after the pile has burst into flames, until the pile of gray ashes is nearly cold. When the pots can be safely handled with bare hands they are removed and inspected.

In general, the Hopis do not use slips on their traditional painted pottery because of the superior quality of the clay. (Slips are solutions of water and clay rubbed on pieces of pottery before polishing.) Paints may be mineral or vegetal. Potters boil down tansy mustard, an herb, to produce a black paint, sometimes adding a bit of hematite. When the vessel is fired, yellow clay becomes a red color, or one of several shades of orange. White pottery is produced from a fine white clay.

The two most common shapes in decorated pottery are a shallow bowl and a flat-shouldered, small-mouthed jar. Usually, decoration is applied to the interior of bowls, and this decoration is asymmetrical. On jars, the design is outside, very symmetrical, and extremely repetitive. Favored themes are birds and parts of birds, such as wings, beaks, and feathers. Additional popular designs are Kachinas, Kachina masks, scrolls, and various geometric elements.

There are a number of prominent Hopi families with a fine legacy and tradition in pottery, such as the family of Grace Chapella, which includes Alma Tahbo, Mark Tahbo, Ethel Youvella, and Verna Nahee. They do beautiful work.

Another such family is the Navasie family, which includes Rainell Naha, Lana David, Dawn Navasie, and the innovative Joy Navasie (Frog Woman) and Helen Naha (Feather Woman).

Joy Navasie's style and technique developed into the use of white slip, a characteristic of her family's pottery. In the past Joy used a flower drawing as her signature, indicating her Hopi name, Yellow Flower. Today she signs her pottery solely with the frog symbol. She feels pleased that the slipped pottery has become recognized. Even though it is difficult to polish the slip, everything else about the Navasie pottery-making process is traditional.

Helen Naha began potting about 1945 in order to help her family with its financial problems. She had to teach herself because she had no teacher to lean on. As a consequence, it took her a long time to learn and it was six years before her pottery began to sell. Even though her husband, Archie, helped with the clay, Helen did most of the work by herself. At first she painted her pottery the way Joy Navasie did. Then she acquired designs from the shards at Awatovi ruins. She and Archie put different designs together, resulting in original combinations. After watching Archie's mother, Paqua, work, Helen began to use a few designs with many variations, though she liked doing the black and white designs the most.

The Nampeyo family includes a long and illustrious roster of exceptional potters. Nampeyo was the first of the Hopi potters to be known and recognized by name. Nampeyo and Maria of San Ildefonso are the best-known of all potters. Their influence has been staggering.

Nampeyo's pottery was characterized by a squat-shaped bowl on which she created her own designs. Nampeyo was eager to teach her family the fundamentals as well as the intricacies of making pottery. She also wanted to hand down the traditional methods and designs, and her descendants have used this legacy in different ways.

Tonita Hamilton Nampeyo doesn't wish to deviate from what her mother, Fannie Polacca Nampeyo, and her grandmother,

Nampeyo, did. She feels the most important thing is to keep tradition alive.

Loren Hamilton Nampeyo learned from being around his grandmother, Fannie, and his mother, Tonita. He also spent a year learning from his uncle, Tom Polacca. He is now potting full time, trying to interpret old designs in his own way.

Tom Polacca, a grandson of Nampeyo, developed his own style of pottery. He introduced the sgraffito method, carving on his pots figures such as Kachinas and animals. Sgraffito is a decorative style produced by cutting away parts of the surface layer of the clay in order to expose a differently colored surface. A very sharp carving knife is used. Remembering all too well the difficulties he had as a self-taught potter, he has chosen to teach other family members.

Tom Polacca taught the sgraffito style to his daughter Elvira Naha Nampeyo, his son-in-law Marty Naha, and daughter Carla Claw Nampeyo. They use Kachina designs, among others. Carla Claw's work is different because she uses a dark brown polished slip on plain seed pots carved with sgraffito. She likes this style because it is unique and modern. Even though her pots are different, they are still done in a traditional form, thereby maintaining the links to her past.

Gary Polacca Nampeyo also learned the sgraffito style of pottery from his father, Tom Polacca. In addition, Gary has come up with some wrinkles of his own. He textures the pot with scenery and colors that are similar to the Hopi landscape. Gary attempts to tell a story with his pottery and

his use of figures, achieving his goal of portraying the ancientness of the Hopi people.

Iris Youvella Nampeyo, a daughter of Fannie, also learned at her mother's knee. The Nampeyo family belongs to the Corn Clan, and when her father asked her to paint corn on a ladle her mother Fannie was working on, Iris thought he meant for her to build up an ear of corn. Years later, this is exactly what she did, with astonishing beauty.

Melda Nampeyo, James Garcia Nampeyo, and Ravin Garcia Nampeyo all tell of the profound influence of their grandmother, Fannie. It was Fannie who encouraged them to stick with pottery and the old traditional designs. In this way they would be able to make a living for their families. This idea was first projected by Nampeyo (Fannie's mother), as she felt it was important for her children to be self-sufficient.

Dextra Quotskuyva Nampeyo, commonly known as Dextra, is the great-granddaughter of Nampeyo. Her shard pots are exceptional—a blending of the old with her innovative designs. She thinks in terms of incorporating the universe—the earth, the sky, human life—into her pottery designs. Dextra encourages other Hopi potters to remember the past as well as to interpret their present dreams in their works. Dextra remembers how blessed the Nampeyo family has been and how profound Nampeyo was in encouraging the family members to become good pottery artists, telling them they were going to survive because of it.

Nampeyo truly began a dynasty of famous pottery artists. Her distinctive style of swirling patterns of birds, butterflies, feathers, and Kachinas has been used by her numerous descendants and students.

There are many fine Hopi potters not from the Chapella, Navasie, and Nampeyo families. There are Garnet Pavatea, Stella Huma, Beth Sakeva, Lawrence Namoki, Otellie and Charles Loloma, and Rondina Huma.

Marcia Fritz Rickey was the daughter of Toonewah, Chief of the First Mesa villages. When Marcia was six years old, her mother, Sally Toonewah, taught her to pot, beginning with very small pieces. Sally never painted her own pots; she just decorated them by pressing her fingernail into the pottery prior to firing. (This became known as the thumbnail design and was also employed by Garnet Pavatea.) When Marcia became older, she made her own pots and painted them using the bold designs found on the shards of the Awatovi ruins. Marcia made very large pots, two to three feet tall, as well as smaller pieces and low bowls. The painting on the inside of her low bowls is outstanding. She would hum and sing while potting, as she said that helped her concentration. Marcia potted until the day she died at the age of seventy-five. She signed her pots with the representation of the Flying Ant.

Elizabeth White was from Old Oraibi on Third Mesa. Polingaysi Qöyawayma was her Hopi name. She was noted for creating a new form with corncobs, and for pressing the clay from the inside to form relief figures of Flute Players. Elizabeth used a potter's wheel and kiln as often as she used the coil method of building her pots and the traditional firing on the ground.

Al Qöyawayma was largely influenced by Elizabeth White, his aunt, who introduced him to the world of pottery. When Al visited with his aunt in her home in Kykotsmovi, he was entranced with her skills and artistry. She taught him how to look for clay, mix it, and experiment with it. Elizabeth told Al that his efforts produced excellent quality and showed that he was aware of what he was doing. Al was delighted by her enthusiasm and acceptance of him as a potter. Over the years Al has become identified with his unusual pots with designs pushed out from the inside. His wares are decorated with bas-relief and repoussé. Very few potters employ these techniques. Even though Al Qöyawayma has had the advantage of a scientific education at universities in California and has worked in Phoenix as a successful scientist, he maintains that he has found the challenge of the clay equal to any experience he had in that world. His pottery is truly elegant and revolutionary.

Pottery is largely considered a woman's craft, but men have certainly made their contribution to the beauty and excitement of Hopi pottery. Al Qöyawayma, Thomas Polacca, Gary Polacca Nampeyo, Wallace Youvella, Mark Tahbo, and Lawrence Namoki are but a few of the men who have carved a distinctive niche.

In an economic sense, the pottery art of the Pueblo Indian is an important industry.

After the pots are fired on the ground, they must cool to minimize cracking.

It not only provides total financial support for hundreds of Indian families, but also furnishes a substantial income for many dealers of Indian art and museum shops throughout the Southwest. The Indian potter now earns a good income, and in the case of better-known potters, a major income. In the world of art the value of a signed piece will appreciate. The Indian potter no longer works at the starvation-level wages of not too many years ago. Indian art has met with growing recognition and acceptance.

Buying pottery is a matter of personal taste. Its variety is immense. Some of the criteria to look for are shape, color, and design. The paint or slip should be applied evenly. It should not appear thin or washed out. Run your hand over the surface to make sure the slipped area is not crazed, cracked, or flaked. The surface of the pot may show fire clouds, discolored, cloudy areas in relation to the rest of the pot, due to uneven heat and oxygen at the time of firing. Generally, fire clouds are not considered desirable; the fewer the fire clouds, the better the quality. In testing the firing quality, tap the rim of the pot with your fingernail. If the pottery is highly fired, it will emit a high-pitched ring. A pot that is cracked will usually give a dull sound when tapped.

The ultimate test in deciding whether or not to buy is your own sense of taste. You should have confidence that the pottery you buy will bring much pleasure from both the beauty of the pot and from the centuries of tradition that lie behind its making.

Is pottery making an art, or is it a craft? In Indian terms there is no such dilemma. The difference can be defined in terms of quality. Any craft object becomes a work of art when exceptional creativity is accompanied with technical skill.

Pottery has been made by the Indians of the Southwest for at least two thousand years. Today pottery is a distinguishing trait of the living Pueblos, and without a doubt it will endure as a beacon of Pueblo vitality and cultural identity. In a sense, making pottery in the traditional way, by hand, without using a machine at all, is really miraculous. The miracle begins with dirt— the clay. Wet it, shape it, and fire it. The soft particles unite to form a strong mass when they cool. Clay becomes pottery. Pottery becomes art.

FROM YEARS PAST, *left to right:*

Canteen, made in 1959 by Elizabeth White.

Wide-mouthed pot incised with running scrolls, ovals, and rectangles, made in 1953 by Otellie and Charles Loloma, kiln fired.

Shallow bowl, made before 1979 by Elizabeth White.

Wind bell with Corn Maiden design and three corn cobs in raised relief, made in 1970 by Elizabeth White.

Courtesy of Museum of Northern Arizona Collection

FROM YEARS PAST:

UPPER ROW, *left to right:* Long-haired Kachina design, by Gary Polacca Nampeyo. *Private collection*

Rain and cloud design, by Garnet Pavatea. *Private collection*

Wedding vase with parrot design, by Helen Naha (Feather Woman). *Private collection*

Parrot design, by Ethel Youvella. *Courtesy of The Galloping Goose*

LOWER ROW, *left to right:* Rain and cloud design, made by Grace Navasie and painted by Joy Navasie (Frog Woman). *Private collection*

Reversible hanging plate with Salako Kachina on one side and an eagle on the other, by Beth Sakeva. *Courtesy of The Galloping Goose*

Rain and cloud design, made circa 1950 by Fannie Polacca Nampeyo. *Private collection*

Prayer feather design, by Marcia Fritz Rickey. *Private collection*

All pottery made in the 1970s, unless otherwise noted.

UPPER ROW, *left to right:* Bird design, by James Garcia Nampeyo.

Rain and cloud design, by Dextra Quotskuyva Nampeyo.

LOWER ROW, *left to right:* Polished pot, by Alton Komalestewa.

Rain and cloud design, by Dextra Quotskuyva Nampeyo.

Private collection

Clockwise from far left: Rain and cloud design,
by Joy Navasie (Frog Woman).

Lizards and corn, by Sylvia Naha.

Turtles, by Sylvia Naha.

Three pots with appliquéd corn design,
by Iris Youvella Nampeyo.

Large pot with rain and cloud design,
by Stella Huma.

Rain and cloud design,
by Joy Navasie (Frog Woman).

Private collection

Clockwise from upper left:

Mud Head Clown, by Tom Polacca.

Warrior Maiden, Aholi Kachina, and Eototo Kachina entitled *Peaceful Solution,* by Lawrence Namoki.

Sun face entitled *Hopi Mystic Entrance,* by Lawrence Namoki.

Pottery Shards, by Loren Hamilton Nampeyo. Sun with pottery shards entitled *My Roots,* by Lawrence Namoki.

Eagle Kachina, by Carla Claw Nampeyo.

Sun with Long-haired Kachina, by Carla Claw Nampeyo.

Salako, by Carla Claw Nampeyo.

CENTER: Velvet Shirt Kachina, by Elvira Naha Nampeyo and Marty Naha.

Courtesy of Monongya Gallery

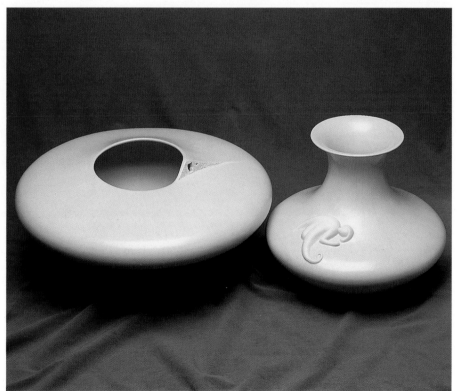

BIRD DESIGNS:

TOP CENTER: Vase-shaped pot made by Emma Naha.

UPPER ROW, *left to right:* Made by Dawn Navasie.

Made by Melda Nampeyo.

Made by Ravin Garcia Nampeyo.

Made by Jacob Koopee Nampeyo.

LOWER ROW, *left to right:* Made by Charlene Kooyaquaptewa.

Made by Dawn Navasie.

Made by Gloria Mahle.

Made by Rosalda Hamilton.

Courtesy of Monongya Gallery

Left to right: Pot with design of ruins.

Pot with One Horn Priest design.

Both made by Al Qöyawayma.

Private collection

Treasures Unlimited

▼ ▼ ▼

THE HOPIS ARE extremely versatile artisans, venturing beyond the parameters of plaques, baskets, jewelry, pottery, and Kachina dolls, the art forms for which they are mainly known. These pages display a panorama of artistic creations—cradleboards, baby quilts, cloth dolls, cradle dolls, gourds and dance rattles, embroidered wedding garments, sashes, and belts. Also featured are tabletas (worn as headdresses in the dances), ankle cuffs, garters, bandoliers, bullroarers, lightning sticks, dance wands, and rabbit sticks. A whimsical wood carving by Rosanda Suetopka is pictured, as well as items made

An assortment of cloth Kachina dolls and clowns, by Vernette Thomas. *Courtesy of Turquoise Village*

of metal, including sculptures of petroglyphs, sophisticated silver boxes, etched zinc engravings by Preston Monongye, sculptured pottery by Kim Obrzut, and the pewter and bronze castings of Kachinas and Hopi legends by Neil David, Sr., and Lowell Talashoma, Sr.

Cotton garments are an integral part of Hopi ceremonial life. Men usually wear embroidered cotton kilts at plaza rituals. The kilt has a broad wool band embroidered with traditional symbols of rain clouds and fields of red, green, and black. A Hopi bride wears both the traditional wedding robe made by the groom and his relatives, and a braided cotton sash. Elaborate symbolic tassels hang from two corners of the robe. A long fringe of white hangs from each end of the sash. The fringe dropping down is a symbol of rain that would be prayed for throughout the life of the bride, so that she and her children might have food. The woman carefully stores her wedding robe all through her life. When she dies the robe will be spread on the ground for her spirit to step upon. In this manner her spirit safely makes its way to the underworld, the spirit home of the Hopis.

Men typically do the weaving among the Hopi Indians. A man sets up the loom in his home or in a kiva. He uses cotton primarily for ceremonial objects, such as the woman's wedding robe and sash, kilts, and embroidered dresses. He uses wool for everyday garments and babies' blankets, maidens' shawls, and rugs. He usually does embroidery and brocading with Germantown wool.

Hopi designs in ceremonial garments tend to be traditional. In embroidered dresses, kilts, and brocaded sashes, cloud and rain themes predominate. The fringed sashes around the waists of the dancers suggest torrential rains. Sprigs of spruce represent rain's generous, benevolent green gifts to the land. Gourd rattles imitate the pattering sound of rain. (Gourds are considered the oldest utilitarian vessel known to mankind.) The ends of the brocaded sash feature additional symbolism. The white zigzag design supposedly represents the teeth of the mountain lion, or those of the Broad-faced Kachina, while the short white parallel marks are the tracks of Pöökanghoya or Taiowa deities.

The tableta is an elaborate, multicolored headdress with symbols designed to produce crops, clouds, rain, rainbows, and corn. Occasionally the tableta suggests phallic symbols for reproduction and fertility. Other tabletas, such as the one with Hano Clowns pictured on page 88, indicate mirth and playfulness. The Hopi girls wear a butterfly tableta in the Butterfly Dance, a social dance during which girls choose their partners from their uncles and nephews.

During dances the Hopis use larger drums to create a timbre of great depth and smaller drums to achieve a muted sound. They use rattles for clear sounds. Almost every dance begins and ends with the signal or the beat of the gourd rattles. There are many different styles and designs of rattles, such as the Buffalo Kachinas, Corn Kachinas, Mud Head Clowns, Flower Kachinas, and even the whimsical, brave title character from *Field Mouse Goes to War.*

To accentuate the desired rhythms, the Hopi dancer wears bandoliers, ankle bands, kilts, belts and knee straps augmented with items that clink, tinkle, or ring when the dancer moves. The turtle shell leg rattle, made of the shell of the desert tortoise, illustrates this type of percussion instrument. The toenails of a sheep or deer are strung and fastened to dangle over the turtle shell. The hollow turtle shell is tied around the back of the dancer's leg, just below the knee. When the dancer walks or stamps his foot, the sheep claws strike the hollow shell, producing a percussive sound. When the dancers do this in unison, it creates a rich, pleasurable, rasping tone.

In the Home Dance the Hemis Kachina is accompanied by the Hemis Kachin-mana, who uses the rasp. This instrument is a gourd shell that rests on the ground. A notched stick is placed on the gourd, and a sheep scapula engages the notched stick, scraping it up and down. This simulates the sound of distant thunder.

The bullroarer is another sound-producing object. It is a small wooden slat with a hole in one end where a six-foot cord is attached. When the bullroarer is whirled in a circular motion, the slat turns, vibrates, and emits a humming sound like distant thunder. The widely held Hopi belief is that this sound brings clouds, lightning, thunder, and rain.

The dancers wear bandoliers that circle over the right shoulder down to the left side of the waist. One type of dance bandolier is a long thin piece of buckskin with attached metal cones or shells. When the dancers move, the bandolier makes a subdued ringing sound.

Many Kachina dancers wear the maiden's shawl as a kilt or a manta. It is woven of coarse cotton or wool. The black and red borders are wool.

The woman's woven belt is extremely colorful—red, black, and green—and has four-inch tassels. Even though it is primarily a woman's belt, many Kachinas wear it in the dances, tying it on the right side.

The ceremonial stockings and leggings worn by many Kachinas are unusual stirrup socks; that is, there is no heel or toe. The white, open-worked socks are knitted from coarse cotton string.

The ceremonial ankle wraps or cuffs are colorful and are approximately four inches wide and fourteen inches long. The base is made of semisoft leather. The dancers wear the cuffs on the bare ankles or as an arm band. The design usually represents a stylized rain cloud.

The paho or prayer stick is a slat of wood made from cottonwood root. Women of the Mamzrau Society carry pairs of prayer sticks as they dance.

The Hopi rabbit stick is used to hunt rabbits. It is shaped like a boomerang and made of hardwood. It is an important implement for securing food. The Makto Kachina has a rabbit stick painted across the face of his white mask.

The lightning stick is carved in a zigzag pattern to represent lightning, and it has triangular points at each end. Kachinas carry it to bring clouds, lightning, and rain.

A newborn Hopi girl receives a flat doll—an image of the Kachina Mother, Hahai-i-Wu-uti—as her first doll. As she grows older, her flat doll presents become more elaborate in facial features and adornments. These are known as cradle dolls.

The following artists are but a small reflection of the abundance of Hopi talent.

The Hopi name of Kim Obrzut is Seyesnem. It means "Fresh Living Flower," a name lovingly bestowed on her by Albert Poleeson, her grandfather. Kim is noted for her contemporary sculptures, done in both ceramic and bronze. Her Hopi Maiden is symbolic of the continuation of life. She is the procreator, the bearer of life. Kim's Maiden has no face, for she symbolizes the equalitarian society of the Hopis. To Kim, the Maiden represents a people, not an individual. The bronze Maiden features a cape as well as corn. Since corn is the basic food of the Hopis, it is considered sacred.

Kim's ceramic pottery is hand coiled and kiln fired. Her venture into bronze casting, with her choice of a slate blue patina, has proven to be exciting and dynamic. Kim Obrzut has won numerous awards at the Museum of Northern Arizona Hopi Show (Flagstaff, Arizona), The Heard Museum (Phoenix, Arizona), The Gallup Inter-Tribal Indian Ceremonial (Gallup, New Mexico), and at Indian Market (Santa Fe, New Mexico).

Vernette Thomas gives all the credit to the making of her whimsical dolls to her son Quinton, who died eleven years ago. Quinton had lung trouble from birth, and the doctors were not able to save him, even with two surgeries. Vernette and Clinton, Quinton's twin, stayed in the hospital for six months until Quinton died.

Vernette became very depressed and was unable to cope with everyday life. One day she had an inner feeling that her dead son, Quinton, told her not to worry about anything and to get on with her life and make dolls, even though Vernette had never thought about doll making. In fact, she hated to sew. She believes that Quinton gave her the gift of making dolls. From that day, she started making cloth dolls and feels as though they are like her own children. She considers them special and never takes shortcuts in the making, using only cloth

and yarn. She feels happy while she is working, and that is why the clowns have big smiles on their faces.

Vernette supports her five children with her work. Her five sons, who range in age from eleven to twenty-three, are helping build a house for the family in Oraibi, Arizona, on Third Mesa.

Howard Sice is a self-taught artisan. He works with jewelry, featuring geometric and rug designs. After experimenting with several finishes, he became well known for the stippling effect he uses on the jewelry. The stippling produces a frosted look, distinguishing it from all other Hopi jewelry. (For an example of this distinctive finish, see page 40 of this author's book, *The Beauty of Hopi Jewelry.*)

In 1990 the Art Commission of the City of Phoenix, Arizona, commissioned Howard Sice to create one hundred medallions of solid copper. Each medallion was a quarter-inch thick and forty inches in diameter, weighing between eighty and one hundred pounds. The medallions are hanging from lampposts on Central Avenue in Phoenix. This project marked the beginning of Howard's interest in metal sculptures. Today he creates Mimbres animals and petroglyphs from steel, then coats them with a reddish-brown copper.

In its May 1996 symposium, the Indian Market in Santa Fe, New Mexico, designated Howard Sice as a Master Artist.

Lowell Talashoma, Sr., is an artist and Kachina doll carver born on the Hopi reservation in Moenkopi, Arizona. In 1983,

Lowell created a carving from cottonwood root of Tutuveni, the Eagle Boy. The carving was then cast in bronze. Titled *Eagle Boy,* the figure is inspired by a Hopi folk tale. In this legend, the eagle transforms the boy into an eagle so that he can fly off the cliff away from his enemies, the boys of his village. The sculpture shows the change in form with a delicacy and pathos.

Neil David, Sr., is a Tewa-Hopi artist born in Polacca, Arizona. Neil, a prolific painter and a renowned Kachina doll carver, is truly an artist raised in a creative culture. He is an initiate to the Kachina Clan and participates in ceremonials as part of his Hopi village life. He is one of the founders of the Artist Hopid group, which existed from 1973 to 1976. Though relatively short in existence, the group has been long in impact and importance to Hopi painting.

Neil's pewter sculpture of a Tewa Clown, entitled *Melon Break*, illustrates his individual sense of humor as well as Hopi humor. His bronze sculpture, *Growing Song*, reflects the spirit of the Long-haired Kachina singing to the corn. The dance and song of the Long-haired Kachina is among the most beautiful performed during the Hopi Kachina cycle.

Rosanda N. Suetopka brings together elements of art and ceremony with daily life. Her cultural heritage is one in which art, religion, and daily thought are inseparable. In her wood statue, *Walk Like an Egyptian*, Rosanda demonstrates that "humor is a universal parallel for all people, that even though we Native Americans have serious religious and cultural responsibilities,

we can't forget that humor is also essential. We must maintain the ability to walk with laughter and grace."

Rosanda has represented the Hopi Tribe at the UNESCO Conference in Sweden on Indigenous Cultures. She also serves as Vice President for the Hopi Board of Education in behalf of the Hopi Tribe.

Her works are shown in galleries across the United States, including the American Indian Contemporary Art Gallery in San Francisco, California, Coconino Center for the Arts in Flagstaff, Arizona, and the Wheelright Museum in Santa Fe, New Mexico.

As these artists and their works demonstrate, there is so much artistry reflecting the life, religion, hope, and culture of the Hopis. One can only wonder what will come next.

FROM YEARS PAST:

An assortment of items worn during the Kachina and social dances from years past:

Hano Clown tableta and Butterfly tableta worn as headdresses, made in the 1970s.

Dance wands of cloud symbols handheld by the Kachinas, made in the 1950s.

Embroidered wedding manta (a dress or robe) of cotton and Germantown yarn, 45½ in. x 74 in., made in 1890.

Embroidered wedding manta, 44½ in. x 65 in., made in 1930.

Orange and green ankle wraps (resting on manta at right), made 1920–1930.

All other ankle wraps were made in 1980s.

White leggings worn in Deer Dance, date unknown.

Butterfly Maiden dance wands, made in 1970s.

Mud Head Clown dance wands, made in 1970s.

Kokopelli Mana dance wands, made in 1990s.

Sash, made in 1972.

Belt, made in 1986 by Willie Coin. The tassels at the ends of the sash and belts symbolize rain.

Corn hoe, made in 1960, representing the cultivation of the corn.

The bandolier with conical shells makes a pleasant sound and is worn on the shoulder of the Kachina. Artists unknown, other than belt, by Willie Coin.

Courtesy of Barbara Goldeen and John Selmer

FROM YEARS PAST:

Cotton and wool shirt, 30 in. x 22 in., aniline dye, dated pre-1958, maker unknown. Patterns are the same as those used in weaving sashes.

Courtesy of Museum of Northern Arizona Collection

FOR THE BABY, FROM YEARS PAST:

Baby quilt, *left,* with village, Long-haired Kachinas, and corn, made in 1989 by Audrey Navasie Tootsie. *Courtesy of Jessica Marie Jensen*

Baby quilt, *right,* with dance rattles and rain and cloud symbols, made in 1991 by Audrey Navasie Tootsie. *Courtesy of James Matthew Jensen*

Wicker cradleboard, made in 1972 by Tillie Mayestewa. *Private collection*

CRADLE DOLLS, *clockwise from upper left:*

Hilili Kachina doll, made in 1974 by Ronald Wadsworth.

Badger Kachina doll, made in 1975 by Ronald Wadsworth.

Rattle Kachina doll, made in 1976 by Gary Calnimptewa.

Ho-ó-te Kachina doll, made in 1976 by Vernon Mansfield.

Sun Kachina doll, made in 1978 by Elaine Tewa.

Harvester Kachina doll, made in 1974 by Ronald Wadsworth.

Corn Kachina doll, made in 1977 by Franklin Namingha.

All cradle dolls are from a private collection

Bench, by Richard Honyouti.

FIRST SHELF ABOVE BENCH, *left to right:* Coil plaque of Butterfly Maiden Kachina, by Lorraine Secakuku. *Courtesy of Von Monongya*

Pot with eagle, by Carla Claw Nampeyo.

Pot with Hano Clown, by Loren Hamilton Nampeyo.

Pot with Kachin-mana, by Marty Naha.

SECOND SHELF ABOVE BENCH, *left to right:* Wicker plaque, artist unknown.

Pot with Hano Mana, by Marty Naha.

Pot with Butterfly Maiden, by Lawrence Namoki.

Pot with Long-haired Kachina, by Carla Claw Nampeyo.

THIRD SHELF ABOVE BENCH, *left to right:* Three belts, by Donald Keevama.

Pot with eagle, by Tom Polacca.

ON THE BENCH, *left to right:* Gourd of Hopi Mana, by Orin Poley, Jr. *Courtesy of Barbara Poley*

Pot with Ahote Kachina and corn, by Tom Polacca.

Gourd of Hopi Mana, by Orin Poley, Jr.
Courtesy of the artist

Pot with insect, by Irma David.

Wedding sash, by Donald Wadsworth.

Large round pot with bird design, by Jacob Koopee Nampeyo.

Pot with bird design, by Dawn Navasie.

White pot with bird design, by Lana David, painted by Joy Navasie.

Gourd of Butterfly Maiden, by Orin Poley, Jr.
Courtesy of Barbara Poley

Wedding sash, by Donald Wadsworth.

ON THE FLOOR, *left to right:* Pot with Long-haired Kachina and turquoise, by Tom Polacca.

Pot with bird design, by Venora Silas.

Pot with bird design, artist unknown.

Pot with bird design, by Claudina Lomakema.

Pot with Butterfly Maiden, artist unknown.

Pot with bird design, artist unknown.

All courtesy of Monongya Gallery, unless otherwise noted

FROM YEARS PAST:

Left to right: Zinc engravings mounted on wood include Corn Yei, 6 in. x 18 in. *Private collection*

Frog and clouds, 2½ in. x 20 in. *Private collection*

Yei with feathers, 2½ in. x 20 in. *Courtesy of Deborah and Dennis Healey*

Long Horn Kachina, 2¾ in. x 20 in. *Courtesy of Deborah and Dennis Healey*

Made in the early 1970s by Preston Monongye.

Note: Measurements are of the zinc engravings without the wood.

Petroglyphs of man and of deer,
steel with copper coating, by Howard Sice.

Courtesy of Museum of Northern Arizona Gift Shop

BRONZES, *left to right:*

Long-haired Kachina and corn entitled *Growing Song*, by Neil David, Sr.

Eagle Boy, by Lowell Talashoma, Sr. Figure is from a Hopi folk tale in which the eagle is turning the boy into an eagle. Note backbone, arm and hand, foot, chest, and wing, showing the transformation in process. *Private collection*

Clockwise from top: Sterling silver box with turtle design, made in 1992 by Bernard Dawahoya. *Courtesy of Heard Museum Gift Shop*

Sterling silver box and lid with Mud Head Clowns, made in 1971 by Loren Sakeva. *Private collection*

Sterling silver box and lid with sun, bear, and bear paws, made in 1973, artist unknown. *Private collection*

ABOVE, *left to right:* Left-handed Kachina, Mother Kachina, Wuwuyoma Kachina, Mother Kachina, Kokopelli Kachina, Corn Kachina, Mud Head Clown. Artists unknown.

Frog Kachina doll (A) with prayer feather, by Ted Puhuyesva.

Lightning sticks (B), bullroarers (C), and rabbit stick (D), artists unknown. The lightning sticks are carried by the Kachinas in the dances to help bring lightning and rain. The bullroarer is whirled in a circular motion making a sound like thunder to help bring rain. The rabbit stick is a throwing stick used to hunt rabbits for food.

Gourd (E) and rasp (F), artist unknown. The gourd is placed on the ground and a sheep's bone is moved along the rasp to simulate the sound of thunder, hopefully to bring rain.

Dance wand of Rain Priest Kachina (G), by Sheldon Talas.

Dance wand of Mud Head Clown (H), by Sheldon Talas.

Dance wands (I), are handheld by the Kachinas in the dances.

Courtesy of Museum of Northern Arizona Gift Shop

CRADLE DOLLS, ABOVE:

Crow Mother Kachina (top left); Broad-faced Kachina (lower left); Early Morning Kachina (left center), by Carla Twoitsie; Ahöla Kachina (right center), by Carla Twoitsie; Spotted Corn Kachina (top right); Sotungtaka Kachina (lower right). All from the 1970s, 1980s, and 1990s. Unless otherwise noted, artists unknown. Cradle dolls are given to the child when it is born and thereafter for several years. *Private collection*

LEFT: Eight dance rattles, by Melvin Yaiva. *Courtesy of Puchteca*

Mother Kachina and Ogre Kachina rattles, by Ted Puhuyesva. *Courtesy of Museum of Northern Arizona Gift Shop*

Five rattles, artist unknown.
Courtesy of Museum of Northern Arizona Gift Shop

Dance rattles, made of gourds, are handheld by the Kachinas in the dances. The dances begin and end with the Kachinas shaking the rattles.

Silver box with14-karat gold, maze design and Kachinas, *clockwise from upper left:* a Long-haired Kachina, a Chasing Star Kachina, an Antelope Kachina, and a Sipikne Kachina, by Joe Josytewa.
Courtesy of Turquoise Village

Walk Like an Egyptian, wood sculpture, 6 ft. 4 in. tall, by Rosanda N. Suetopka. This won first prize at the Museum of Northern Arizona Hopi Show in Flagstaff in 1987. The inspiration of this sculpture to Rosanda came from a satire that a Tsuku (yellow clown) did at a summer Kachina dance in the village of Hotevilla. It showed her that in spite of the oppression that Hopi and other Native American tribes have endured throughout the centuries they have an ability to laugh at themselves and with each other. *Courtesy of the artist. Leg belts hanging from the neck and the waist of the sculpture (artist unknown) are courtesy of Museum of Northern Arizona Gift Shop.*

Maidens, by Kim Obrzut, are hand coiled and kiln fired. Kim states that the maidens she creates are symbolic of the continuation of life since women are the procreators, the bearers of life. Her maidens have no faces, symbolizing the equalitarian society of the Hopi. The maidens represent a people, not an individual. Her venture into bronze has been very dynamic with the slate blue coloring.

Left to right. Bronze Hopi Maiden with cape and corn. *Private collection*

Pottery Hopi Maiden with plaque. *Courtesy of the artist*

Pottery Hopi Maiden with headdress of cloud symbol. *Courtesy of the artist*

Melon Break, pewter sculpture of Tewa clown, by Neil David, Sr. *Private collection*

MELON BREAK

GLOSSARY

▼▼▼

BANDOLIER A piece of buckskin with attached metal cones or shells, worn across the chest of the Kachinas in the dances. It makes a ringing sound.

BOLA TIE A leather tie with a jeweled ornament.

BULLROARER A stick that is whirled in a circular motion, making a sound like thunder to help bring rain.

CONCHA BELT A belt made from oval or round silver discs.

DREMEL An electric power tool used in the carving of Kachina dolls.

FIRE CLOUDS A different coloration on a piece of pottery due to a piece of burning fuel touching the pot.

GOURD AND RASP The gourd is placed on the ground and a sheep's bone is moved along the rasp to simulate the sound of thunder, with the hope of bringing rain.

KACHINA A supernatural being that is an intermediary to the Gods. Also, a masked dancer representing that being.

KACHINA DOLL A doll made from cottonwood root depicting a certain Kachina.

KILN An enclosure for firing pottery.

KIVA An underground ceremonial chamber.

KOSHARI A clown.

KOYEMSI A clown.

LIGHTNING STICK A wooden stick with lightning designs carried by the Kachinas in the dances to help bring lightning and rain.

MANTA A textile worn over the shoulders. Also, a dress or robe.

NIMAN DANCE The last Kachina dance before the Kachinas go home to the San Francisco Peaks.

OVERLAY Two sheets of silver soldered together in the making of Hopi jewelry.

PAHO A prayer stick or prayer feathers sometimes carried by the Kachinas in the dances.

PETROGLYPH An ancient carving in rock, usually a rock wall, of animals or figures.

PIKI A wafer-thin Hopi bread.

PIKI TRAY A woven tray on which the piki is stacked.

POWAMU Sometimes called the Bean Dance, this ceremony is held in February.

RABBIT STICK A throwing stick used to hunt rabbits for food.

REPOUSSÉ Pressing or hammering out a design from the underside of jewelry or pottery.

SGRAFITTO A decorative style produced by cutting away parts of a surface layer of the clay in order to expose a different colored surface.

SHARDS Broken pieces of pottery.

SLIP A solution of water and clay rubbed on a piece of pottery before polishing.

SOYAL CEREMONY The winter solstice ceremony in which the Kachinas come into the villages for the first time. During this ceremony the kivas will be opened.

SPLIT-TWIG FIGURINES These were originally made of wood and were first discovered in a side canyon in the Grand Canyon. They are estimated to be 2,500 to 8,000 years old.

TABLETA or **TABLITA** A wooden headdress worn in the Kachina and Social dances.

TEMPER A fine sand or pulverized shards mixed with clay to reduce the possibility that a pot may crack during firing.

TIHÜ Another name for a Kachina doll.

X-ACTO KNIFE A very sharp-bladed tool used in the carving of Kachina dolls.

SUGGESTED READING

▼▼▼

Adair, John. *The Navajo and Pueblo Silversmiths.* University of Oklahoma Press. Norman, Oklahoma. 1944.

"Arizona Living Treasure Award." *The Indian Trader* newspaper, July 1992. Gallup, New Mexico.

Bahti, Mark. *Pueblo Stories and Storytellers.* Treasure Chest Publications, Inc. Tucson, Arizona. 1988.

Bahti, Tom. *Southwestern Indian Tribes.* K. C. Publications. Las Vegas, Nevada. 1968.

Barry, John W. *American Indian Pottery.* Books Americana, Inc. Florence, Alabama. 1981.

Bartlett, Kathleen. "Hopi and Hopi-Tewa Pottery." *Plateau Magazine,* 1977. Museum of Northern Arizona. Flagstaff, Arizona.

Bassman, Theda. *The Beauty of Hopi Jewelry.* Kiva Publishing, Inc. Santa Fe, New Mexico. 1993.

———. *Hopi Kachina Dolls and their Carvers.* Schiffer Publishing Ltd. West Chester, Pennsylvania. 1991.

———. *The Kachina Dolls of Cecil Calnimptewa Their Power Their Splendor.* Treasure Chest Publications. Tucson, Arizona. 1994.

Bedinger, Margery. *Indian Silver Navajo and Pueblo Jewelers.* University of New Mexico Press. Albuquerque, New Mexico. 1973.

Belknap, Bill. *Fred Kabotie: Hopi Indian Artist.* Museum of Northern Arizona with Northland Press. Flagstaff, Arizona. 1977.

Bennett, Edna Mae and John F. *Turquoise Jewelry of the Indians of the Southwest.* Turquoise Books. Colorado Springs, Colorado. 1973.

Broder, Patricia Janis. *Hopi Painting: The World of the Hopis.* E. P. Dutton. New York. 1978.

Bunzel, Ruth L. *The Pueblo Potter.* General Publishing Company. Toronto, Ontario, Canada. 1929.

Byron, Harvey. *Dancing Kachinas: A Hopi Artist's Documentary.* Heard Museum of Anthropology and Primitive Art. Phoenix, Arizona. 1971.

Cirillo, Dexter. *Southwestern Indian Jewelry.* Abbeville Press Publishers. New York. 1992.

Colton, Harold S. *Hopi Kachina Dolls with a Key to Their Identification.* University of New Mexico Press. Albuquerque, New Mexico. 1959.

Cohen, Lee M. *Art of Clay.* Clear Light Publishers. Santa Fe, New Mexico. 1993.

Dillingham, Rick. *Fourteen Families in Pueblo Pottery.* University of New Mexico Press. Albuquerque, New Mexico. 1994.

———. *Seven Families in Pueblo Pottery.* University of New Mexico Press. Albuquerque, New Mexico, 1974.

Dockstader, Frederick J. *The Kachina and the White Man.* University of New Mexico Press. Albuquerque, New Mexico. 1985.

———. *Indian Art in North America.* New York Graphic Society. Greenwich, Connecticut. 1961.

Earle, Edwin and Edward A. Kennard. *Hopi Kachinas.* Museum of the American Indian, Heye Foundation. New York. 1971.

Eaton, Linda B., PhD. *Native American Art of the Southwest.* Publications International, Ltd. Lincolnwood, Illinois. 1993.

Feder, Norman. *American Indian Art.* Harry N. Abrams, Inc. New York. 1965.

Fergusson, Erna. *Dancing Gods.* University of New Mexico Press. Albuquerque, New Mexico. 1931.

Furst, Peter T. and Jill L. *North American Indian Art.* Rizzoli International Publications, Inc. New York. 1982.

Gill, Spencer. *Pottery Treasures.* Graphic Arts Center Publishing Co. Portland, Oregon. 1976.

Goddard, Pliny Earle. *Pottery of the Southwestern Indians.* The American Museum of Natural History. New York. 1928.

Harlow, Francis H. *Modern Pueblo Pottery.* Northland Press. Flagstaff, Arizona. 1977.

Jacka, Jerry and Lois Essary. *Beyond Tradition.* Northland Publishing Co. Flagstaff, Arizona. 1988.

Jacobs, Martina Magenau. *Kachina Ceremonies and Kachina Dolls.* Carnegie Museum of Natural History, Carnegie Institute. Pittsburgh, Pennsylvania. 1980.

Johnson, Sandy. *The Book of Elders.* Harper. San Francisco, California. 1994.

Kennard, Edward A. *Field Mouse Goes to War.* Bureau of Indian Affairs. United States Department of the Interior. 1944.

Manley, Ray. *Ray Manley's Portraits & Turquoise of Southwest Indians.* Ray Manley Photography, Inc. Tucson, Arizona. 1975.

———. *Ray Manley's Southwestern Indian Arts & Crafts.* Ray Manley Photography, Inc. Tucson, Arizona. 1975.

Mason, Otis Tufton. *Aboriginal Indian Basketry.* The Rio Grande Press. Glorieta, New Mexico. 1970.

Monthan, Guy and Doris. *Art and Indian Individualists.* Northland Press. Flagstaff, Arizona. 1975.

Museum of Northern Arizona. *The Basket Weavers: Artisans of the Southwest.* Museum of Northern Arizona. Flagstaff, Arizona. 1982.

O'Kane, Walter Collins. *The Hopis: Portrait of a Desert People.* University of Oklahoma Press. Norman, Oklahoma. 1953.

———. *Sun in the Sky.* University of Oklahoma Press. Norman, Oklahoma. 1950.

Page, Susanne and Jake. *Hopi.* Harry N. Abrams, Inc. Publishers. New York. 1982.

Ricks, Brent J. and Alexander E. Anthony, Jr. *Kachinas: Spirit Beings of the Hopi.* Avenyu Publishing, Inc. Albuquerque, New Mexico. 1993.

Tack, Alan. "Book Review." *Native Peoples Magazine,* Winter 1992. Phoenix, Arizona.

Tanner, Clara Lee. *Ray Manley's Hopi Kachinas.* Ray Manley Photography, Inc. Tucson, Arizona.

———. *Southwest Indian Painting.* University of Arizona Press. Tucson, Arizona. 1973.

———. *Southwest Indian Craft Arts.* University of Arizona Press. Tucson, Arizona. 1968.

———. *Indian Baskets of the Southwest.* University of Arizona Press. Tucson, Arizona. 1983.

Teiwes, Helga. *Kachina Dolls: The Art of Hopi Carvers.* The University of Arizona Press. Tucson, Arizona. 1991.

Toulouse, Betty. *Pueblo Pottery of the New Mexico Indians.* Museum of New Mexico Press. Santa Fe, New Mexico. 1977.

Trimble, Stephen. *Talking with the Clay.* School of American Research. Santa Fe, New Mexico. 1987.

Tryk, Sheila. *Santa Fe Indian Market.* Tierra Publications. Santa Fe, New Mexico. 1993.

Turnbaugh, William A. and Sarah Peabody Turnbaugh. *Indian Jewelry of the American Southwest.* Schiffer Publishing, Ltd. West Chester, Pennsylvania. 1988.

Vroman, Adam Clark. *Dwellers at the Source.* Grossman Publishers. New York. 1973.

Wilson, Maggie. "Man, Myths, and Rituals." *Arizona Highways,* September 1979. Phoenix, Arizona.

The World of the American Indian. National Geographic Society. Washington, D.C. 1958.

Wormington, H. M. and Arminta Neal. *The Story of Pueblo Pottery.* Denver Museum of Natural History. Denver, Colorado. 1951.

Wright, Barton. "Kachina Carvings." *American Indian Art Magazine,* Spring 1984. Scottsdale, Arizona.

———. *Clowns of the Hopi.* Northland Publishing. Flagstaff, Arizona. 1994.

———. *Hopi Kachinas The Complete Guide to Collecting Kachina Dolls.* Northland Press. Flagstaff, Arizona. 1977.

———. *Hopi Material Culture.* Northland Press. Flagstaff, Arizona. 1979.

———. *Kachinas: A Hopi Artist's Documentary.* Northland Publishing. Flagstaff, Arizona. 1973.

———. *The Unchanging Hopi.* Northland Press. Flagstaff, Arizona. 1975.

Wright, Margaret Nickelson. *Hopi Silver.* Northland Publishing. Flagstaff, Arizona. 1972.

Young, John V. *Kokopelli.* Palmer Lake, Colorado. 1990.

INDEX OF ARTISTS

▼▼▼

Acadiz, Lawrence, 28, 36
Adams, Maggie, 49
Ami, Carletta, 37

Bahnimptewa, Clifford, 31, 55–56, 60
Begaye, Nathan, 71

Calnimptewa, Cecil, 30
Calnimptewa, Gary, 89
Calnimptewa, Vernon, 34
Chapella, Grace, 73
Coin, Willie, 13, 31, 88
Coochwykvia, Marcus, 15
Coochwytewa, Victor, 9–10, 14, 17

Dallas, Effie, 44
Dallas, Logan, 55, 58
David, Irma, 90
David, John, 28, 35
David, Lana, 73, 90
David, Neil, Sr., iv, 56–57, 61, 64, 65, 83,
      87, 92, 96
Dawahoya, Bernard, 9, 92
Dawahoya, Bueford, 12, 21
Dawahoya, Dinah, 12, 21
Dawangyumptewa, David, 57, 69
Dextra. *See* Nampeyo, Dextra Quotskuyva
Duwyenie, Preston, 15

FCT, 18
Feather Woman. *See* Naha, Helen
Flying Ant. *See* Rickey, Marcia Fritz
Fred, Aaron, iv
Fred, Julian, 18, 19
Fred, Perry, 19, 21
Fredericks, Aaron, 28, 36
Frog Woman. *See* Navasie, Joy

Hamilton, Rosalda, 81
Hamna, Walter, 31
Hawee, Billy Rae, 14
Heveniyowma, 31
Holmes, Emery, 19
Holmes, Ernie, 38
Honanie, Delbridge, 56
Honanie, Jimmie Gayle, Sr., 27, 33

Honanie, Phillip, 9–10, 11, 13, 19
Honanie, Tirzah, iv, 49, 50
Honanie, Watson, 9–10, 23
Hongeva, Leroy, 38
Honhongva, Sherian, 11
Honie, Norman B., 13
Honivisiona, Randall, 13
Honyaktewa, Leroy, 15, 18, 21
Honyaktewa, Robert, 15
Honyouti, Brian, 27–28, 38
Honyouti, Richard, 90
Hoyungowa, Manuel, 7
Huma, Rondina, 71, 75
Huma, Stella, 75, 79

James, Eldon, 9, 14
Joshevama, Patrick, 36
Josytewa, Guy, 15
Josytewa, Joe, iv, 12, 15, 20, 95
Josytewa, Marsha, 12, 15

Kabotie, Alice, iv, 9
Kabotie, Fred, 8–9, 10, 13, 29, 53–54,
      55, 56, 58, 62
Kabotie, Michael, 56, 67
Kaye, Peggy, 41, 48
Kaye, Wilfred, 28, 35
Kaye, Wilson, 32
Keevama, Donald, 90
Koinva, Elliot, 18, 19
Koinva, Lucion, 15, 18
Komalestewa, Alton, 78
Koopee, Jacob, 25
Kootswatewa, D'Armon, 27, 36
Kooyamoema, Martha Leah, 50
Kooyaquaptewa, Charlene, 81
Kooyaquaptewa, Sherry, 37
Kuwaninvaya, Cedric, 22
Kuwanvayouma, Terrance, 18
Kyasyousie, Raymond, 12, 18, 19, 22

Laban, Brian, 27, 39
Lacapa, Elizabeth, 57
Lacapa, Michael, 57, 66
Lamson, Janet, 49
Lamson, Madeline, 49, 50

Lamson, Shannon, 14
Lanyade, 7
Lesso, 72
Loloma, Charles, 9–11, 22, 75, 77
Loloma, Otellie, 75, 77
Lomadopki, Robert, 23
Lomahongva, Edward, 19
Lomakema, Claudina, 90
Lomakema, Leon, 19
Lomakema, Milland, 56
Lomakema, Zola, 49
Lomakewa, Corbin, 17
Lomawywesa. *See* Kabotie, Michael
Lomayaktewa, Harold, iv, 15
Lomayaktewa, Moody, 17, 21
Lomayestewa, McBride, 12, 18
Lomayesva, Reuben, 57
Lomayesva, Walden, 57
Lucas, Dawn, 15, 19
Lucas, Dorothy, 17
Lucas, Glenn, 10, 13, 21
Lucas, Kenny, 25, 32
Lucas, Marvin, 17
Lucas, Trinidad, 17, 18

Mahkee, Patricia, 35
Mahkee, Vern, 28, 35, 37, 39
Mahle, Gloria, 81
Maktima, Duane, 9–10, 12, 13
Mansfield, Verden, iv, 12, 15, 21
Mansfield, Vern, 12, 15, 20, 21
Mansfield, Vernon, 89
Maria of San Ildefonso, 73
Mayestewa, Tillie, 47, 89
Monongye, Preston, 9–10, 14, 83, 91
Mootzka, Waldo, 54–55, 62

Naha, Archie, 73
Naha, Emma, 81
Naha, Helen, 73, 78
Naha, Marty, 74, 80, 90
Naha, Neal, Jr., 64
Naha, Rainell, iv, 73
Naha, Raymond, 54, 57, 59
Naha, Sylvia, 79
Nahee, Orme, 34

Nahee, Verna, 73
Namingha, Dan, 53, 57
Namingha, Franklin, 89
Namingha, Raymie, 15, 17
Namingha, Wayland, 34
Namoki, Hyram, 29, 35
Namoki, Lawrence, 36, 41, 75, 80, 90
Namoki, Watson, 37
Nampeyo, 57, 71, 72, 73–75
Nampeyo, Bonnie, 37
Nampeyo, Carla Claw, 37, 74, 80, 90
Nampeyo, Dextra Quotskuyva, 57, 74, 78
Nampeyo, Elvira Naha, 41, 74, 80
Nampeyo, Fannie Polacca, 73–74, 78
Nampeyo, Gary Polacca, 74, 75, 78
Nampeyo, Iris Youvella, iv, 74, 79
Nampeyo, Jacob Koopee, 81, 90
Nampeyo, James Garcia, iv, 74, 78
Nampeyo, Loren Hamilton, 74, 90
Nampeyo, Melda, 74, 81
Nampeyo, Neva, 34, 41
Nampeyo, Priscilla N., 34, 41
Nampeyo, Rachel, 57
Nampeyo, Ravin Garcia, 74, 81
Nampeyo, Tonita Hamilton, 71, 73–74
Navasie, Dawn, 73, 81, 90
Navasie, Grace, 78
Navasie, Joy, 73, 78, 79, 90
Navasie, Muriel, 28
Nequatewa, Jack, 15, 17
Nequatewa, Verma, 11
Nutima, Frank, 13
Nutumya, Adrinne, 48
Nuvamsa, Pascal, 15

Obrzut, Kim, 83, 85–86, 96

Pahona, Cordilla, 57
Paqua, 73
Pavatea, Garnet, 75, 78
Pawiki, Richard, 17
Pela, Evelyn, 50
Phillips, George, 18, 20
Phillips, Loren, 14, 18
Polacca, Tom, 74, 75, 80, 90
Poleahla, John, 33

Poleahla, Randolph, iv
Polelonema, Otis, 54, 60
Polelonema, Tyler, 56
Poleviyouma, Jacob, 14
Poley, Orin, Jr., 90
Pooyouma, Gene, 10
Poseyesva, Philbert, 9–10, 17, 20
Puhuhefvaya, Fernando, 17, 20, 21
Puhuyesva, Ted, 93, 94

Qöyawayma, Al, 75, 81
Qöyawayma, Polingaysi. See White, Elizabeth
Quanimptewa, Harvey, Jr., 17
Quannie, Kevin Horace, 28, 35
Quiyo, Louis, 18
Qumyintewa, Alde, 18
Quo-ma-hong-ka, 31
Qwavenka, Ida, 31

Rickey, Marcia Fritz, 75, 78
Robinson, Morris, 13

Sakeva, Beth, 75, 78
Sakeva, Dora, 49
Sakeva, Loren, 92
Saufkie, Andrew, 19
Saufkie, Lawrence, iv, 12, 13, 17, 18
Saufkie, Paul, Jr., 8, 13, 54
Saufkie, Ruben, 21
Saufkie, Von, iv
Secakuku, Lorraine, 29, 49, 51, 90
Secakuku, Sidney, 12
Sehongva, Merle, 19
Sekaquaptewa, Emory, 9
Sekaquaptewa, Wayne, 9
Selestewa, Leonard, 28, 34
Seyesnem. See Obrzut, Kim
Shelton, Henry, iv, 28, 31
Shelton, Mary, 28, 36
Shelton, Peter, 9, 32
Sice, Howard, 86, 91
Sikiumptewa, 13
Sikyatala, 7
Silas, Venora, 90
Sockyma, Mitchell, 23

Sonwai, 9–10, 11, 22. See also Honhongva,
    Sherian; Nequatewa, Verma
Sosolda, Alvin, 20
Suetopka, Roger, 27, 32
Suetopka, Rosanda N., 83, 87, 95
Supplee, Charles, 9–10, 11, 22

Tahbo, Alma, 73
Tahbo, Mark, 73, 75
Talaheftewa, Roy, 9–10, 12, 22
Talas, Sheldon, 37, 93
Talashoma, Lowell, Sr., 83, 86–87, 92
Talaswaima, Terrance, 56
Tawahongva, Berra, 19
Tawahongva, Duane, 17
Taylor, Eli, 38
Taylor, Milson, 12, 23
Tewa, Dennis, 27, 38
Tewa, Elaine, 89
Tewa, Orlando, 35
Tewawina, Beatrice, 50
Thomas, Vernette, 83, 86
Timeche, Bruce, 55, 63
Timeche, Porter, 10
Toonewah, Sally, 75
Tootsie, Audrey Navasie, 89
Touraine, Pierre, 11
Twoitsie, Carla, 94

Wadsworth, Donald, 90
Wadsworth, Ronald, 21, 89
Wadsworth, Ted, 13
White, Elizabeth, 75, 77

Yaiva, Melvin, 94
Yellow Flower. See Navasie, Joy
Yestewa, Cheryl Marie, 9–10, 21
Youvella, Ethel, 73, 78
Youvella, Tino, 32
Youvella, Wallace, 75
Yowytewa, Art, 34

GENERAL INDEX

▼▼▼

Ahöla Kachina, 30, *31, 36, 94*

Ahote Kachina, 30, *90*

Ahülani Kachina, *36*

American Indian Contemporary Art
    Gallery, 87

Angwusi Kachina, 30

Angwusnasomtaqa Kachina, 30

Ankle wraps, 85, *88*

Antelope Kachina, *95*

Anthony, Alexander, Jr., 56–57

Apache Kachina, 30, *39*

Arizona Indian Living Treasures Award, 28

Art forms, 83, *88. See also* Baskets and
    basketry, Jewelry, Kachinas, Pottery,
    Plaques

Artist Hopid, 56

Awatovi, 2

Baby accessories, *89*

Bacavi, 1, 42

Badger Kachina, *89*

Bandoliers, 85, *88*

Basket Dance, 43

Baskets and basketry, *ii, iv,* 31, 40, 41–45,
    46–51
    coil, 43–44, *49, 50, 51*
    colors, 42–44
    design motifs, 42, 43, 44
    Hopi prominence, 41–42, 45
    and loom work, 41
    plaiting, 41–42
    ring baskets, 42
    selection guidelines, 45
    shapes, 43
    sifter baskets, *40,* 41, 42, *46, 47*
    warp and weft, 41
    weavers, 44–45
    wicker weaving, 42–43

Bean Dance, 26, 43

Bears and bear paws, *6, 7, 14, 15, 16,* 17, *18,
    19, 23*

Belt buckles, *ii, iv, 6, 7, 13, 20, 21*

Belts, 13, 85, *88, 90*

Bench, 90

Bird designs, *70,* 71, *78, 81, 90*

Black Ogre Kachina, *24, 25,* 30

Blankets, *31*

Bola ties, *6, 7, 13, 14, 18, 19*

Bow guards, *13*

Bracelets, *ii, iv, 6, 7, 14, 15, 19, 20, 22*

Broad-faced Kachina, *13, 17, 94*

Bronze work, *92, 96*

Buffalo Kachinas, 84

Bullroarers, 85, *93*

Butterfly, *48, 50, 88*

Butterfly Dance, 84

Butterfly Girl, 30, *35*

Butterfly Kachina Maiden, 30, *31, 49, 69,
    88, 90*

Buttons, *13*

Canteen, *77*

Carvers and carving, 26, 27–28, 83, 86–87

Chapella family, 73, 75

Chasing Star Kachina, 30, *32, 95*

Chusona Kachina, 30

Clay, 71–72

Cloud design, *15, 49, 88, 91*

Clowns, *82,* 83. *See also* Hano Clowns,
    Kaisale Clown, Mud Head Clowns,
    Tewa Clowns

Coconino Center for the Arts, 87

Coil plaques, *iv, vi, 40,* 41, 44, *49, 50, 90.
    See also* Miniature coil plaques

Colton, Harold, 7–8, 55

Colton, Mary Russell, 7–8

Concha belts, *17*

Corn Clan, 74

Corn Dance Leader Kachina, *iv, viii, 17*

Corn designs and symbols, *18, 19, 21, 79*

Corn hoe, 88

Corn Kachina, *17,* 84, *89, 93, 94*

Corn Maiden Kachina, *17, 77*

Corn Yei, *91*

Cotton garments, 83–84

Cradleboard, *89*

Cricket Kachina, *17, 48*

Cross-legged Kachina, 30, *31, 32, 38*

Crow Kachina, 30, *37*

Crow Mother Kachina, *iv, vi, 16, 17,* 30, *37,
    44, 48, 51, 94*

Cuff links, *19*

Dances, 2–3, 26. *See also* Basket Dance, Bean
    Dance, Butterfly Dance, Deer Dance,
    Home Dance, Kachina dance cere-
    monies, Line Dances, Mixed Dances
    accessories, 84–85, 93

Deer, *50*

Deer Dance, 88

Deer Kachinas, *ii, iv, 15*

Dolls, ii, iv, *94. See also* Kachinas—dolls

Dragon Fly Kachina, *17*

Dunn, Dorothy, 55

Eagle Boy, 87, *92*

Eagle Kachina, viii, *17, 32, 36, 38, 51, 80*

Eagles, *ii, iv, viii, 21, 90,* 30, *32, 36, 38, 49,
    50, 78*

Early Morning Kachina, *48, 94*

Earrings, *6, 7, 13, 18, 20, 22, 23*

Eight Antelope Singers, 60

Emergence of Cloud Woman, 64

Engravings, *91*

Eototo Kachina, *17*

Fewkes, J. W., 71–72

Field Mouse Goes to War, 28–29, 84

First Mesa, 1, 7, 71, 75

Flower Kachinas, 84

Fred Harvey Co., 54

Frog Kachina, *93*

Frogs, *91*

Gallup Inter-Tribal Indian Ceremonial, 35,
    49, 86

Gold, 8, 10, 12, *22, 23*

Gourds and gourd rattles, 84, *90, 93, 94*

Grand Canyon, 22

Great Horned Owl Kachina, 30, *33*

Growing Song, 87, *92*

Guardian of the Children, 64

Hahai-i-Wu-uti Kachina, 85

Hair pieces, *19*

Hano (Tewa), 1, 71

Hano Clown Kachinas, 30, *37,* 84, *88, 90*

Hano Mana Kachina, 30, *34, 38*

Harvester Kachina, *89*

Heard Museum, 86
Heheya Kachinas, *17*, 30, *37, 49*
Hemis Kachina, iv, *viii*, 85
Heye Foundation, 54
Hilili Kachina, iv, *vi*, 89
Hólolo Kachina, 30, *31*
Home Dance, 26–27, 85
Ho-ó-te Kachina, 21, 30, *89*
Hopi
    clans, 3
    crafts, 5
    culture, 2, 4–5, 54
    current population, 1
    dry farming, 1–2
    and education, 4
    G.I. training program, 8
    households, 3
    humor, 29
    land holdings, 1, *4*
    matriarchal society, 3
    and outside world, 4
    "people of peace," 5
    as Pueblo Indians, 1
    religion, 2–3, 26
    and Spanish missionaries, 2
    villages, 1
Hopi Arts and Crafts Silvercraft Cooperative
Guild, 8–9
Hopi Board of Education, 87
Hopi Bringers of Rain, 61
Hopi Cultural Center Museum, 56
*Hopi Kachina Dolls with a Key to Their
Identification*, 55
Hopi Show (Museum of Northern Arizona),
57, 95
Hopi Way, 10
Hopi Women's Basket Dance, 62
Hopicrafts, 9
Hornet Kachina, 30, *37*
Hotevilla, 1, 11, 42
Hotsko Kachina, 30
Huhuwa Kachina, 30
Hump-backed Flute Player Kachina, *17, 21,*
    30, 75
Hunter Kachina, *17, 48*

Jewelry, 7–12, 86. *See also* Hopi Arts and
Crafts Silvercraft Cooperative Guild,
Hopicrafts
    artists, 9–10
    overlay, 7–8, 11–12
    silversmithing, 7, 9, *92, 95*

Kachina Cult, 26
Kachina dance ceremonies, 2–3, 26, 43
Kachina Maiden, 30, *39*
Kachinas, 25–29, 57
    Ahöla, 30, *31, 36, 94*
    Ahote, 30, *90*
    Ahülani, *36*
    Angwusi, 30
    Angwusnasomtaqa, 30
    Antelope, *95*
    Apache, 30, *39*
    Badger, *89*
    Black Ogre, *24*, 25, 30
    Broad-faced, *13, 17, 94*
    Buffalo, 84
    Butterfly Kachina Maiden, 30, *31, 49, 69,*
        88, 90
    carvers and carving, 26, 27–28
    Chasing Star, 30, *32, 95*
    Chusona, 30
    cloth, *82, 83*, 86
    Corn, *17*, 84, *89, 93, 94*
    Corn Dance Leader, iv, *viii, 17*
    Corn Maiden, *17, 77*
    Cricket, *17, 48*
    Cross-legged, 30, *31, 32, 38*
    Crow, 30, *37*
    Crow Mother, iv, *vi, 16, 17*, 30, *37,* 44,
        48, 51, 94
    Deer, *ii*, iv, *15*
    dolls, *ii*, iv, *vi*, 25–26, 27–29, *31–39, 82,*
        83, 89
    Dragon Fly, *17*
    Eagle, viii, *17, 32, 36, 38, 51, 80*
    Early Morning, *48, 94*
    Eototo, *17*
    erotic, 29
    Flower, 84
    Frog, *93*

Great Horned Owl, 30, *33*
Hahai-i-Wu-uti, 85
Hano Clowns, 30, *37,* 84, *88, 90*
Hano Mana, 30, *34, 38*
Harvester, *89*
Heheya, *17*, 30, *37, 49*
Hemis, iv, *viii*, 85
Hilili, iv, *vi*, 89
Hólolo, 30, *31*
Ho-ó-te, 21, 30, *89*
Hornet, 30, *37*
Hotsko, 30
Huhuwa, 30
Hump-backed Flute Player, *17, 21*, 30, 75
Hunter, *17, 48*
as intermediaries to the gods, 25
Kachin-mana, *18*, 30, *48, 49, 90*
Kaisale, 30
Kaisale Clown, *36*
Kau-a Kachina, 48
Kokopelli, *6, 7, 8, 14, 16, 21, 23*, 30, *36,*
    68, 69, 93
Kokopölö Mana (or Kokopelli Mana), *17,*
    88
Koshare, 29, 30
Koyemsi, *17, 29*, 30
Koyona, 30
Kwa, 30
Kwasa-itqa, 30
Kweo, 30
Kwikwilyaqa, 30
left-handed, 30, *50, 63, 93*
list of, 30
Long-haired, *15, 17, 18, 19, 21, 49, 61,*
    67, 78, 80, 87, *89, 90, 92, 95*
Long Horn, *91*
Makto, 85
masks, 27, *59*
Mastof, 30, *32*
Mocking, 30, *32*
Mongwa, 30
Mother, *35, 48, 49*, 85, *93, 94*
Mud Head Clowns, *ii*, iv, *14, 18, 19*, 30,
    34, 36, 37, 49, 50, 51, 80, 84, *88, 92, 93*
Na-ngasohu, 30
Nata-aska, 30

Navan, 30
Niman, 26–27
Ogre, *60, 94*
Ota, 30
Palhik Mana, 30
Paralyzed, 30, *36*
Patun, 30
Planet, 30
Polik Mana, 30
Rain Priest, *93*
Salako, iv, *vi, 17,* 30, *35, 50, 51, 64, 78, 80*
Salako Mana, *ii,* iv, 30, *35*
Salako Taka, *ii,* iv, 30, *35*
Screech Owl, 30, *31*
Sipikne, *95*
Situlilü, 30, *36*
Skirt Man, 30, *32*
Snow Maiden, *ii,* iv, *48*
Sotungtaka, *94*
Squash, 30, *34, 36*
    as spirit beings, 25
Sun, 30, *38, 89*
Supai Girl, *49*
Suy-ang-e-vif, 30
Takus Mana, 30
Tata-nga-ya, 30
Tawa, 30
Tewa Clowns, *65,* 87, *96*
Tühavi, 30
Turkey, 30, *34*
Velvet Shirt, 30, *36, 80*
Warrior Maiden, *80*
White Ogre, *24,* 25, 30, *39*
Wolf, 30, *31, 36*
Wuwuyoma, *93*
Yellow Ahote, *38*
Yellow Corn Girl, 30
Yellow Corn Maiden, 30, *35, 38*
Yoche, 30
Zuni Rattlesnake, 30
Kachinas: A Hopi Artist's Documentary, 56
Kachinas: Spirit Beings of the Hopi, 56–57
Kachin-mana Kachina, *18,* 30, *48, 49, 90*
Kaisale Kachina, 30
Kaisale Clown Kachina, *36*

Kau-a Kachina, *48*
Kennard, Edward A., 29
Key holders, *19*
Kilts, 83, 84, 85
Kivas, 3, 26, 56
Kokopelli Kachina, *6, 7, 8, 14,* 16, *21, 23,* 30, *36, 68, 69, 88, 93*
Kokopölö Mana (or Kokopelli Mana) Kachina, *17*
Koshare Fiesta, 62
Koshare Kachina, 29, 30
Koyemsi Kachina, *17,* 29, 30
Koyona Kachina, 30
Kwa Kachina, 30
Kwasa-itqa Kachina, 30
Kweo Kachina, 30
Kwikwilyaqa Kachina, 30
Kykotsmovi, 1, 9, 42, 57, 75

Left-handed Kachinas, 30, *50, 63, 93*
Lefties and Hunting, 63
Leggings, 85, *88*
Life cycle design, *6, 7*
Lightning sticks, 85, 93
Line Dances, 26
Lizards, *79*
Long-haired Kachinas, *15, 17, 18, 19, 21, 49, 61, 67, 78, 80,* 87, *89, 90, 92, 95*
Long Horn Kachina, *91*

Maidens, *96. See also* Butterfly Kachina Maiden, Corn Maiden, Kachina Maiden, Snow Maiden KachinaWarrior Maiden, Yellow Corn Maiden
Makto Kachina, 85
Mamzrau Society, 85
Mason, Otis Tufton, 45
Mastof Kachina, 30, *32*
Maze designs, *20*
Melon Break, 87, *96*
Midday Sun, 68, 69
Miniature coil plaques, *ii,* iv. *See also* Coil plaques
Mishongnovi, 1, 43
Mixed Dances, 26
Mocking Kachina, 30, *32*

Moenkopi, 1, 42
Money clips, *19*
Mongwa Kachina, 30
Mother Kachina, *35, 48, 49,* 85, *93, 94*
The Mud Head Clown, 60
Mud Head Clown Kachinas, *ii,* iv, 14, 18, 19, 30, *34, 36, 37, 49, 50, 51,* 80, *84, 88, 92, 93*
Museum of Northern Arizona, 7–8, 57, 86, 95
Museum of the American Indian, 54

Nampeyo family, 73, 75
Na-ngasohu Kachina, 30
Nata-aska Kachina, 30
Navan Kachina, 30
Navasie family, 73, 75
Necklaces, *6, 7, 13, 21*
New Oraibi, 9
Niman Kachina, 26–27

Ogre Kachina, *94*
Ogre Woman, 60
One Horn Priest, *81*
Oraibi, 1, 42, 55, 75, 86
Oraibi High School, 54, 56
Ota Kachina, 30
Overlay, 7–8, 11–12

Pahos, 85
Paintings, *52, 53–57, 58–69*
Palhik Mana Kachina, 30
Paralyzed Kachina, 30, *36*
Parrots and parrot design, *15, 18, 21, 70, 71, 78*
Patun Kachina, 30
Pendants, *13, 14, 16, 17, 20, 22, 23*
Petroglyphs, *91*
Phoenix, Arizona
    Art Commission, 86
    Indian School, 55
    Sky Harbor International Airport, 57
Piki, 3–4
    stone, 3
    trays, *31,* 42
Pins, 13, 14, 16, 17, 20
Plaiting, 41–42

Planet Kachina, 30
Plaques, 41–45, 90
    coil, iv, *vi, 40,* 41, 44, *49, 50*
    miniature coil, *ii,* iv
    and wedding ceremony, 43
    wicker, *46, 47*
Polacca, 1, 71
Poleeson, Albert, 85
Polik Mana Kachina, 30
Polik Mana Watching the Frogs Go By, 69
Pottery, *ii,* iv, *40,* 41, *70,* 71–77, *75, 77,*
    78–81, 86, *90, 96*
    buying, 76
    coil and scrape method, 72
    craft vs. art, 77
    firing, 72
    Hopi clay, 71–72
    as industry, 75–76
    miniature, *34, 37*
    painting, 72–73
    sgraffito, 74
    shapes, 73
    Sikyatki, 8, 71
    Sikyatki Polychrome, 71
    slips, 72, 73
    thumbnail design, 75
Powamu, 26
Prayer feather design, 78
Prehistoric Petroglyph Mogollon Imagery, 66
Pueblo Rebellion, 2

Quilts, *89*

Rabbit sticks, 85, 93
Rain and cloud design, *15, 50, 51, 70,* 71, *78,*
    79, 89
Rain Priest Kachina, *93*
Rain Spirits, 67
Rasps, *93*
Ricks, Brent, 56
Ring baskets, 42
Rings, *13, 14, 15, 22, 23*
Roadrunner, *19*
Rocky Mountain Sheep Dancers, 58

Salako Kachina, iv, vi, *17, 50, 51, 64, 78, 80*

Salako Mana Kachina, *ii,* iv, 30, *35*
Salako Taka Kachina, *ii,* iv, 30, *35*
Salakos, 30, *35*
San Francisco Peaks, 25
Santa Fe, New Mexico
    Indian Market, 57, 86
    Indian School, 54–55
School of American Research, 53–54
Screech Owl Kachina, 30, *31*
Sculpture, 83, 85–86
Second Mesa, 1, 8, 43, 53, 56, 57
Shirt, *88*
Shungopavi, 1, 2, 43, 53, 54, 55
Sichmovi, 1, 7, 71
Side Dancers, 26
Sifter baskets, *40,* 41, 42, *46, 47*
Sikyatki Butterflies Symbolic Imagery, 66
Sikyatki Polychrome, 71
Sikyatki pottery, 8, 71
Silversmithing, 7, *92, 95*
Sipaulavi, 1, 43
Sipikne Kachina, *95*
Situlilü Kachina, 30, *36*
Skirt Man Kachina, 30, *32*
Smithsonian Institution, 28
Snake Dance at Old Oraibi, 55
Snake Dancers, 21, 30, *31, 36, 58*
Snakes, 21
Snow Maiden Kachina, *ii,* iv, *48*
Sotungtaka Kachina, *94*
Soyal, 26
Split-twig jewelry, *22*
Squash Kachina, 30, *34, 36*
Star design, *50*
Sun face and sun, 14, *17, 18, 19,* 30, *38,*
    21, 80, 89
Sun Kachinas, 30, *38, 89*
Supai Girl Kachina, *49*
Suy-ang-e-vif Kachina, 30

Tabletas, 83, 84, *88*
Takus Mana Kachina, 30
Tata-nga-ya Kachina, 30
Tawa Kachina, 30
Tewa Clowns Kachina, *65,* 87, *96*
Third Mesa, 1, 11, 42, 43, 55, 75, 86

Thomas, Clinton, 86
Thomas, Quinton, 86
Tihü, 26
Toonewah, 75
Tühavi Kachina, 30
Turkey Kachina, 30, *34*
Turtles, *ii,* iv, *50, 79, 92*

The Underwater People, 69
UNESCO Conference on Indigenous
    Cultures, 87

Velvet Shirt Kachina, 30, *36, 80*

Walk Like an Egyptian, 87, *95*
Walpi, 1, *5, 52,* 53, 71
Walpi Night Dance, 52, 53
War God, iv, *vi, 49*
Warrior Maiden Kachina, *80*
Warrior Mouse, 28–29, 30, *35*
Watchbands, *14, 19*
Water design and symbol, *15, 16, 18, 19, 23*
Water spirits, 69
Weaving, 84
Wedding mantas, *88*
Wedding sashes, *90*
Wedding vase, 78
Wheelright Museum, 87
White Ogre Kachina, *24,* 25, 30, *39*
Wolf Kachina, 30, *31, 36*
Wood carving. *See* Carvers and carving
Wright, Barton, 56
Wuwuyoma Kachina, *93*

Yava, Albert, 29
Yeis, *91*
Yellow Ahote Kachina, *38*
Yellow Corn Girl Kachina, 30
Yellow Corn Maiden Kachina, 30, *35, 38*
Yoche Kachina, 30

Zuni, 7
Zuni Rattlesnake Kachina, 30

ABOUT THE AUTHOR

THEDA BASSMAN was led by back-packing and river-running exploits into Arizona and New Mexico, where she was pleased to find that her feelings for nature and the environment were rather similar to those expressed by many Native Americans of the region. She developed many friendships within the Native American communities in a short period of time. For the past fifty years she has traveled to Indian lands in the Southwest, not only to visit her friends but to buy their crafts. In 1972 she opened a gallery in Beverly Hills, California, called The Indian and I. When she and her husband retired, they moved to Palm Desert, California, where they now live. They also have a cabin on the Mogollon Rim in northern Arizona, where they spend their time in the forest and traveling to the nearby Indian reservations. Theda has judged Indian shows at the Museum of Northern Arizona in Flagstaff, Arizona; the Gallup Inter-Tribal Indian Ceremonial in Gallup, New Mexico; the Santa Fe Indian Market in Santa Fe, New Mexico; the O'Odham Tash in Casa Grande, Arizona; and the American Indian and Western Relic Show in Pasadena, California. Theda Bassman is a feminist, an environment-alist, and a lover of chamber music. She is a member of Greenpeace, the Sierra Club, and the Hemlock Society, and is a Hospice volunteer.

ABOUT THE PHOTOGRAPHER

GENE BALZER is a professor of photography at Northern Arizona University in Flagstaff. He has photographed most of the collection of the Museum of Northern Arizona, also in Flagstaff, and conducts field trips to various archaeological sites and national parks on the Colorado Plateau. Balzer's photographs have appeared in *Arizona Highways, American Indian Art Magazine, Southwest Profile, Plateau* magazine, *The World and I*, and *The Indian Country Guide*. One of his photographs was featured on the cover of a compact disc by Native American flutist R. Carlos Nakai. Balzer is the photographer for all of Theda Bassman's books.